Dear Gail and (   )

Christmas Presence

CANDY ABBOTT

WITH CONTRIBUTIONS BY
MEMBERS AND FRIENDS OF

DELMARVA CHRISTIAN WRITERS' FELLOWSHIP

We wanted to send you my poem,
"The Piece-able Kingdom"
to share the Peace of the Christmas message.
With our love to our brother and sister,
Kathy (now a published poet ☺)

and   Harry (her lifelong supporter ☺)

CHRISTMAS PRESENCE
Copyright © 2013 Candace F. Abbott

ISBN 978-1493521005 soft cover
ISBN 978-1-886068-73-5
Christian Life • Religious and Inspirational
Personal Growth • Faith • Self-Help

Published by Fruitbearer Publishing, LLC
P. O. Box 777, Georgetown, DE 19947
302.856.6649 • FAX 302.856.7742
www.fruitbearer.com • info@fruitbearer.com

Cover Illustration and Graphic Design by Candy Abbott
Editing and Proofreading by Wilma Caraway

Printed in the United States of America

Christmas Presence

CANDY ABBOTT

WITH CONTRIBUTIONS BY
MEMBERS AND FRIENDS OF
DELMARVA CHRISTIAN WRITERS' FELLOWSHIP

Dedicated

To readers
who know how to sense Christ's presence
in the beauty, delights, and depths
of all that is Christmas.

Introduction

Jesus is always with us, whether we're singing sacred Christmas carols to honor His birth or enjoying festivities with our children like visiting Santa. We may not see the Lord with our physical eyes, but if we are sensitive to the Holy Spirit, we can sense His presence right there in the room with us, maybe even looking over our shoulder—certainly hearing every word we say and seeing everything we do.

The little girl on the cover, who is fairly gasping for breath as she spiels off her wish list to Santa, is unaware of Jesus' presence. But He cares for everything that concerns her and is, even now, monitoring every aspect of her life. How do I know? Because that little girl is me. The watercolor painting is a self-portrait based on a black-and-white department store photo from 1954.

With the help of Delmarva Christian Writers' Fellowship, I have compiled this family-friendly Christmas book, which contains a variety of stories, devotionals, poems, puzzles, and tidbits we trust will enhance your Christmas experience this year and for years to come.

Established in 1993, Delmarva Christian Writers' Fellowship (DCWF) meets the third Saturday of every month in Tunnell Hall at the Georgetown Presbyterian Church, 203 North Bedford Street, Georgetown, Delaware, from 9 a.m. to 12:30 p.m. Meeting attendance runs from eight to twenty-eight. Many are new writers who are mentored by those who have been published. It is an informal gathering for critiquing and encouragement with resources to build up the Christian who writes. There is no membership fee, no formal agenda, and no pressure, but we do hold one another accountable to see progress in our writing. Meetings typically include a devotional, shared information, a teaching, manuscript critiques, and prayer. Friendships are fostered over lunch and between meetings. On occasion, we host day-long writing seminars or retreats and encourage participation in other local/regional/national conferences.

This compilation of Christmas stories, devotionals, poems, and tidbits is our third publication. The first, *CHRIST IS NEAR: Advent Meditations* by Delmarva Christian Writers' Fellowship, was initially published in 2002 to give beginning writers an opportunity to see their work in print. Eight years later, it was completely revised, and the second edition was released in 2011. In 2012, *Christmas,* a 142-page anthology was released, and we extended the opportunity for submission of manuscripts to friends of our writers' fellowship.

Since the inception of DCWF, many of our members have progressed in their writing, and two new groups have been formed: *Vine & Vessels Christian Writers Fellowship* (which meets the fourth Saturday of the month and hosts an annual conference), and *Kingdom Writers Fellowship* (which meets the third Tuesday evening of each month). Some of our members have relocated or passed away, and new members have joined our fellowship. The collection you hold in your hand is a small representation of the many writers who have been encouraged and who have encouraged others in their quest to write with excellence and delight, to the glory of God.

We hope you enjoy this family-friendly Christmas book. Who knows? Maybe it will spark a desire in you to write!

For more information, visit www.DelmarvaWriters.com, or call Candy Abbott, director, at 302.856.6649.

Table of Contents

Christmas Presence

Our Christmas Gift

Ruth Thomas

❦

In a humble stable small
was born the Son of Man.
Angels heralded him to earth
to bring salvation's plan.

Two thousand years have come and gone
since that manger scene.
It's been replaced within our world
with lights of red and green.

Gifts and trees and Santa Claus
is what our children know.
They seldom hear of God's great gift
so many years ago.

A greater gift was never known,
nor love so strong and true,
Than that displayed by Jesus Christ
who died for me and you.

The world may have its Santa Claus,
its glitter and its glow.
But they have missed the greatest gift—
The Savior that we know.

Candy Abbott

The clank of the metal door and the echo of their footsteps rang in the ears of Ivy and Joanne as they walked down the dingy corridor behind the prison guard toward the "big room." The aroma of Ivy's homemade chocolate chip cookies wasn't enough to override the stench of ammonia from the recently mopped floor or the bitterness and anger that hung in the air. Women's Correctional Institute was not the kind of place where seventeen-year-olds go for an outing, but Ivy had a mission.

She was a new believer, and the Scripture, "When have you visited me in prison?" grabbed her heart. She didn't know what she was getting into, but she had to try. Several weeks ago, with trembling fingers, she had dialed the number for an appointment at the prison. Warden Baylor was receptive to Ivy's desire to visit and referred her to Joanne, another teen who had expressed interest.

"How do we do this?" Ivy asked.

"Who knows? Maybe homemade cookies would break the ice," Joanne suggested.

So they baked their cookies and here they were, bearing gifts to strangers.

"I put almonds in these," Ivy rambled nervously as they moved along. "The dough was gummier than usual . . ."

"Don't chatter," the guard snapped. "It gets the prisoners riled."

The harsh words made Ivy jump and her heart pound. She walked the rest of the distance in silence.

"Okay. Here we are," the guard grunted, keys rattling. "You go in. I'll lock the door behind you. Be careful what you say. They have a way of using your words against you. You have fifteen minutes. Holler if you have any trouble." Ivy noted the prisoners' orange jumpsuits and felt overdressed. *Maybe we shouldn't have worn heels*, she thought. *They probably think we're snobs.*

Remembering the guard's admonition, the girls put the cookies on the table next to plastic cups of juice without a word. Some prisoners leaned against the wall; others stood around. Watching. Studying. Thinking. Staring. Nobody talked. Ivy smiled at one of the women, and she scowled back. From then on, she avoided eye contact. After five minutes of strained silence, Joanne whispered, "Let's move away from the table. Maybe they'll come over."

As they stepped back, one of the prisoners blurted out, "I'm gettin' a cookie." The others followed and began helping themselves. Soon they heard the rattle of keys. Time was up.

"What a relief to get outta there," Joanne sighed as a gust of fresh air caressed their perspiring faces.

"Yeah," Ivy agreed. "But there's a tug inside me that we're not done. Would you be willing to go back?"

Joanne nodded with a half-smile. "How about Thursday after school?"

Week after week they came. And week after week the prisoners ate the cookies, drank the juice, and stood around in silence. Gradually, antagonistic looks were replaced by an occasional smile. Still, Ivy couldn't bring herself to speak—not a word.

Then one Thursday, just before Christmas, an evangelist walked in. Her step was sure, her chin was high, and she glowed with the love of God. But she meant business. "I've come to pray with you," she announced. "Let's make a circle."

Ivy was awed by the inmates' compliance. Only a few resisted. The others, although murmuring, inched their way toward the middle of the room and formed a lopsided circle, looking suspiciously at one another.

"Join hands," the evangelist instructed. "It's not gonna hurt ya, and it'll mean more if you do." Slowly they clasped hands, some grasping hard, others barely touching. "Now, bow your heads." Except for the orange outfits, it could have been a church meeting.

"Okay. We're gonna pray," she continued, "and prayer is just like talking, only to God. I want to hear you tell the Lord one thing you're thankful for. Just speak it out. Don't hold back."

Ivy's palms were sweaty. *I can't pray out loud, Lord. I can't even talk to these women. Guess I should set an example, but they probably don't even like me—think I'm better than them 'cause of my clothes.*

The words of an inmate jolted her from her thoughts.

"I'm thankful, God, for Miss Ivy bringing us cookies every week."

Another voice compounded the shock, "God, thanks for bringing a black lady to see us, not just Quakers and Presbyterians."

Ivy's eyes brimmed with tears as she heard, "Thank you, God, for these two ladies givin' their time every week even though we can't do nothin' to pay 'em back."

One by one, every inmate in the circle thanked God for Ivy and Joanne. Then Joanne managed to utter a prayer of gratitude for the prisoners' words. But when it came Ivy's turn, she was too choked up to speak. Her eyes burned in humble remorse over how wrong she'd been about these women. She wished she could blow her nose, but the inmates were squeezing her hands so tightly, she resorted to loud sniffles and an occasional drip.

The following week, Ivy and Joanne returned, bright-eyed, to find the prisoners talkative.

"Why *do* you bring us cookies every week?" a husky voice inquired from the corner of the room. When Ivy explained, she inched a few steps closer. "Can you get me a Bible?" she asked. Others wanted to know more about the Jesus who inspires teenagers to visit prisoners.

A ministry was born from Ivy's cookies. What started as a silent act of kindness and obedience turned into a weekly Bible study at the prison which eventually grew so big it split into several groups that continue to this day. After Joanne married and moved away, Ivy continued to minister to the inmates alone for years. Eventually, Prison Fellowship picked up the baton.

Ivy is a Grandmom now. Her radiance has increased with age, and she brightens any room she enters. But last Thursday afternoon she indulged herself in a good cry. Curled up on the couch, wrapped in the afghan her daughter had made, she wept. Deep sobs wracked her body as she remembered it had been one year since her daughter died of asthma. She ached over the loss and felt, for the first time, the full weight of her words, "The kids can live with me." The baby was asleep in his crib and the two girls were in school when the doorbell rang.

There stood a young woman, probably 17, with a plate of home-made cookies.

"Are you Ivy Jones?" she asked.

"Yes," she answered, dabbing her eyes with a wadded tissue.

"These are for you," the girl said as she handed the cookies to her with a shy, sad smile, turning to leave without another word.

"Thank you," Ivy whispered in a daze. The girl was halfway down the sidewalk when Ivy called out, "But why?"

"My grandmother gave me her Bible before she died last week, and her last words were, 'Find Ivy Jones and take her some homemade cookies.'"

As the girl walked away, a wave of precious memories, uncertainties and younger days flooded Ivy's soul. Swallowing the lump in her throat, she choked back a sob and headed toward the phone. *It's been a long time since I talked with Joanne.*

"Ivy's Cookies" has been previously published in:
Chicken Soup for the Prisoner's Soul
Chicken Soup for the Christian Woman's Soul
Stories for a Woman's Heart
Stories for a Teen's Heart 2
Small Acts of Grace

This Season

Michele Jones

It's not about the tinsel
It's not about the lights
It's not about some reindeer
that flies the skies at night
It's not about the Jones'
and all that "keeping up"
It's not about the bikes or games
and all that other "stuff"

It's about one truth
A message given to us
since the prophets of old
Restoration and redemption for our souls
A message and revelation to us of love
sent down to mankind from the Father above

It's about the truth of our life's plan
and the future of all man
That has been so carefully mastered
from the beginning
It's about an unfathomable love
for all His children
An uncomprehending love
that is never ending

For God so loved the world
that He sent His only Son
To save us from our wayward selves
to restore us to the Father as one

Wise men traveled from far
Seeking this truth
guided by one brilliant star
Which shown brightly before them
and guided their way
They traveled to honor the Christ child
born of lowly estate

Gifts three did they bring to honor a king
Gold from their wealth, a mighty treasure
His gift to us we can never measure
Frankincense given to a little child
So young and innocent and meek
His Word and Spirit of Truth
Is our fragrance sweet
And the gift of myrrh
His death proclaiming
The ultimate price for our redeeming

Redemption's child
our coming King
It's about the help for the one in need
It's about the hope for the orphan's cry
and the widow's plea
It's about a Christ child
who is Savior and is King
With great power and might does forever reign
And who has promised
is coming again

So faith child
every day is our season
Not just one day out of the year
We must spread this gospel story
So that the truth will reach every ear
Don't just see a tiny baby
neatly tucked and fast asleep
See a risen Savior born for you and me
See Him in all His splendor
He is our LORD and our KING!

Merry Christmas

David Michael Smith

There's a little girl trembling on a cold December morn,
Crying for Momma's arms,
At an orphanage just outside a little China town,
Where the forgotten are.
But half a world away,
I hang the stockings by the fire,
And dream about the day,
When I can finally call you mine.
It's Christmastime again but you're not home,
Your family is here and yet you're somewhere else alone,
So tonight I pray that God will come and hold you in His arms,
And tell you from my heart, I wish you a Merry Christmas.

Over and over and over again the results came back . . . negative. Always negative. Weeks turned to months and then to years as my wife and I desperately tried to do what God intended happily married couples to do, procreate, start a family. But after too many failures to list, including unsuccessful artificial inseminations, fruitless in vitro fertilization procedures, heart wrenching miscarriages, enough ovulation kits to move the stock price, visits to doctors and specialists and half the country praying for my wife, Geri, and me, we were still childless after ten years of marriage. We were frustrated and depressed. We felt incomplete, even empty.

Holidays were particularly humbling. Our families would gather for gifts at Christmas, or on birthdays, and our nephews and nieces always commanded center stage. We missed being part of that fun and frivolity. On Christmas morning, my wife and I exchanged gifts, but we dearly missed the pitter patter of small feet excitedly running around the house with the new toys Santa had delivered the eve before.

Although we had discussed adoption on numerous occasions, particularly after being told by expert physicians we were unable to conceive, we never seemed to be on the same page with the solution. When Geri was ready, I questioned my motives. When I was ready, she was unsure of her inner feelings. We both agreed to wait until we were both on board, totally, completely, for the sake of the child. That child would need our unconditional love and devotion, and this endeavor could not be taken lightly. So we continued to lift the idea up in prayer.

And then one day, in about as anticlimactic fashion possible while driving to work, I casually asked my wife if she'd like to adopt a little girl from China and she immediately shouted, "Yes!" I was ready, in my heart, mind, and spirit. There were no reservations whatsoever. God had answered our prayers. We were going to be parents!

The process to adopt internationally was a long, tedious process, nearly fifteen months in length from the initial overview meeting to the time we traveled to China. Mountains of paperwork, consultations with counselors, social case workers and agency representatives, scheduling passport photos *(twice)* and background checks; it wore us out. And the entire time, we never knew who our daughter would be. She was this faceless, nameless child somewhere in the third largest country in the world, one little soul in a nation of 1.3 billion persons. But we knew she had been abandoned and needed a mommy and daddy. Then, around Christmas in 2003 we met with our agency representative in Newark, Delaware.

"I have something you're going to be very excited about . . . your daughter," she said with a smile.

She produced a letter sized manila envelope and slid it across the polished wooden table to us. We sat there in silence staring at it. The woman left the room, granting us privacy, and my wife emptied the contents of the envelope. There was minimal information printed across a single page listing our daughter's Chinese name, probable date of birth, and the Southeastern China orphanage where she resided. Two photographs, both face down, spilled onto the table. Forgetting to breathe, we flipped them over and for the very first time saw the face of our daughter. Tears filled our eyes as we stared blankly at the images of this petite cherub-faced child, jet black hair, and round dark eyes staring into the camera.

Her name was Ji Hua Chen, but we already knew her as Rebekah Joy Smith. We would later keep part of her Chinese name, Ji, as a second middle name. In only five months, we would fly to bring this girl home, her permanent family home.

After our visit with our representative, we drove back to our quiet house to trim our Christmas tree and prepare to celebrate the holiday season, our final one without our tiny daughter.

As I hang the tinsel on the tree and watch the twinkling lights,
I'm warmed by the fire's glow,
Outside the children tumble in a wonderland of white,
And make angels in the snow.
And half a world away you try your best to fight the tears,
And hope that heaven's angels come to carry you here.
It's Christmastime again but you're not home,
Your family is here and yet you're somewhere else alone,
So tonight I pray that God will come and hold you in His arms,
And tell you from my heart, I wish you a Merry Christmas.

Our first Christmas with Rebekah in 2004 was wonderful, despite the fact she was sick with a runny nose. Many of the Christmas morning photographs captured a nose redder than Rudolph's. And being only 18 months old, she didn't fully grasp the concept of opening presents, usually more entertained by the empty box than what was inside. But joy reigned over our household that season, and we were thankful for our family. Life was good; God was good.

And then my wife discovered she was pregnant. Suspicions were confirmed by a pediatrician's foolproof blood test, and every visit after that confirmed the baby was in perfect health. We rejoiced! The first time we heard the baby's heartbeat on the ultrasound, we wept. We also learned we would have a son—Matthew Robert Smith, his middle name coming from his paternal grandfather who would die from lung cancer prior to the baby's birth. Rebekah was going to have a little brother to grow up with.

It was November, with Rebekah's second Christmas with us only a month away and Matthew three months in the womb of life, when my father died peacefully with the family gathered at his bedside.

Until then, Rebekah had been struggling to take her first steps. Several weeks of failed attempts had passed. But that very night after dinner something magical happened . . . she walked. She was overjoyed at her strong, confident steps. And with this newfound mobility, Rebekah's second Christmas brought those pitter pattering feet to our home.

It's Christmastime again and now you're home,
Your family is here so you will never be alone,
So tonight before you go to sleep, I'll hold you in my arms,
And tell you from my heart, I wish you a Merry Christmas!

Song 41106, Merry Christmas, written by Brad Avery, David Carr, Mac Powell, Mark Lee, Tai Anderson, Copyright © 2006 Consuming Fire Music (ASCAP), used by permission of Capital CMP Publishing.

The Christmas Gift

Mary Emma Tisinger

For God so loved the world, that he gave his one and only Son . . .
John 3:16a NIV

It was two days before Christmas, and there I was, in a department store doing last-minute Christmas shopping. It had been a dreary, cloudy December day, and I was tired, unhappy, and frustrated with not being ready for the holidays. And, no luck this evening. I had not been able to find that "just right" gift I was searching for.

As I was leaving the store, I saw her—an elderly woman with a shopping cart just outside the door, ready to enter. Hurriedly, I opened the door, but she backed away, pointing to the big red sign, E-X-I-T, above the door. Still wanting to help, I opened the adjacent door. Her face glowed with a warm smile, but it was her words that warmed my heart. "Thank you," she said. "God bless you."

Suddenly, it seemed the sun was breaking through the clouds. My inner connector, my direct line to God, buzzed loudly as her words echoed in my ears. *She asked you to bless me, Lord, and she's a perfect stranger! And, it made me feel good!*

Red poinsettias, lined up against the wall, caught my eye and reminded me of the reason I was in the store—to search for a special gift to show my love. We were celebrating God's gift to the world—to show how much He loves us—with the birth of a Baby in a manger in Bethlehem many years ago. That gift was Jesus, the Son of God, born to be the Savior of the world.

And just now, this lady had shared God's love with me with those three little words, *God bless you.* It was a gift . . . a Christmas gift.

I smiled. "You are welcome," I replied, and we went our separate ways, she with her shopping cart, and I, clutching my unexpected Christmas gift tightly to my heart.

Thank you, Lord, for reminding me
that the greatest gift we can give one another
is the gift of love.

In the presence of hope —
Faith is born.

In the presence of faith —
Love becomes a possibility!

In the presence of love —
Miracles happen!

Dr. Robert H. Schuller
from *The Be (Happy) Attitudes*

Joy Puzzle... Jesus is Born!

Anonymous

An activity for families to do together. Complete the puzzle by looking up the Scripture verses below to find words that describe Jesus.

<u>DOWN</u>

1. Job 19:25
2. John 4:25
4. Isaiah 7:14
6. Isaiah 9:6
7. Deuteronomy 18:15
8. Isaiah 9:6
9. Luke 2:11
12. Psalm 24:7

<u>ACROSS</u>

3. Isaiah 9:6
5. Isaiah 11:1
10. Isaiah 42:6
11. Numbers 24:17
13. Isaiah 9:6

Answer Key

(No peeking until after you've looked up the verses and filled in the boxes!)

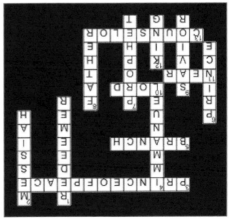

Rebirth of a Dream

Dan Hayne

We married later in life. I was 50 years old and Ruth had just turned 43. Even though we were both getting older, we had a strong desire to become parents and raise our child to know Jesus. After nearly two years of trying with no results, we went to a fertility specialist who ran several tests. His diagnosis was not what we expected. "Your window of opportunity to have children is pretty much closed," he told us. Our balloon nearly burst.

Three months came and went. Ruth was driving home and stopped to make a left turn into the entrance of our apartment complex when a young man crashed into the rear of her car. Ruth was pretty shaken up, because the gentleman was traveling at about 30 miles per hour when he collided with her. After a ride to the hospital in an ambulance, Ruth had X-rays, an MRI, and medication for back pain. Ruth was released from the hospital later that night and came home very stiff and sore from the collision.

Two days later, I received a phone call from Ruth while I was driving home from work. She told me that she had followed a prompting to take a home pregnancy test. Amazingly, the test revealed that Ruth was pregnant! A flood of emotions shot through both of us. We were finally going to be parents at the ages of 45 and 53. Ruth quickly made an appointment with a doctor and discovered she was about six weeks into her pregnancy. News of our miracle spread quickly through our family and circle of friends.

Another two days passed, and Ruth began having symptoms that pointed to something being terribly wrong with her pregnancy. A trip to the hospital confirmed that she was in the beginning stages of a miscarriage. Had the pain medications or X-rays caused this? We prayed fervently for a couple more days, hoping against hope that God would somehow intervene and reverse the diagnosis. Then the unthinkable happened. Ruth was taking a shower, and I heard a wail come from the bathroom. She had just miscarried. We were dumbfounded and devastated.

We initially felt that our miscarried child was a girl. A few days later, a picture passed through Ruth's mind. The picture was of a young boy dressed in white with a white bow tie, sitting in a white room joyfully swinging his legs while sitting on a white cube. We tried to find some comfort in the message of the image Ruth saw. Was this a picture of our miscarried child in heaven? But, wasn't he supposed to be a girl?

Now, it seemed as though our desire to have our own children would never happen. As far as we were concerned, our dream had died. Trying to come to grips with this, we thought we could impact someone else's child in a positive way through foster parenting. So, we took the next step and became licensed foster care parents. A short time later, a case worker dropped off a three-month-old baby boy and his sister of fifteen months. The sudden addition to our family was challenging, but very rewarding to say the least.

After several months, another case worker arrived at our door to send our foster children to another home. It happened very suddenly with only a couple hours warning. I was still at work when all this happened, and I didn't get to say good bye to our foster children. At the time, Ruth and I were so devastated, we were unable to see God's hand at work.

We decided to travel to Florida to visit my mother and let our minds clear up from all we had been through the past few years. Paul, a good friend of our family, prayed for Ruth and me. As he finished, Paul said he believed God was going to give us a child of our own.

Afterwards, Paul's wife pulled him aside and asked him in a serious tone, "Are you *really sure* God said that?"

After all, Ruth and I were getting older.

Much to everyone's surprise—especially ours—within days Ruth conceived again! At this time she was 47 and I was 55. However, several weeks later, Ruth realized she had the symptoms of yet another miscarriage. Shaken to the core, we had close friends at our church pray for us. Miraculously, just a few days afterward, everything returned to normal. There were no more complications from that point on, and the pregnancy went to full term. With complete amazement and joy, we found ourselves holding our own healthy baby boy in our arms.

Fast forwarding three years, Ruth had recently come to the realization that the picture she saw of the young boy wearing white must have been of our son in heaven just before she became pregnant with him. As she explained this insight to us at the breakfast table, our son, who had just turned three years old added, "An angel carried me."

Ruth and I both sat there stunned as we realized that our son had just described a wonderful journey where an angel carried him from heaven and delivered him into Ruth's womb at the point of his conception. Eager to uncover more details, I asked our son if the angel who carried him had wings. He quickly gave a straightforward response, "No, he was a *regular* angel."

Even though we had given up on the possibility of having our own child, God gave us the precious gift of our son who is now more than four years old. What a joy he has been to us. And what an amazing thing to think that God cares for us enough to bring a dead dream back to life.

> *But the angel said, "Don't be afraid, Zacharias!*
> *For I have come to tell you that God has heard your prayer."*
> Luke 1:13 TLB

One Christmas Morning

Teresa D. Marine

My brother, Chris, and I had torn through all our Christmas gifts, and brightly colored paper, ribbons and bows littered our living room floor. Mom came in and saw the clutter and said, "Okay, Dawn, let's put everything neatly back under the Christmas tree so all our gifts will look nice when the rest of the family gets here."

Mom arranged my stand-up doll next to its bright maroon case, which held her clothes and shoes. Then she placed our games and my fire-engine-red wagon beneath the tree; but when she reached for my book, I clung tightly to it.

"Please, Mommy. I want to keep reading."

She smiled and winked at me. "You can as soon as we finish organizing our gifts."

"Mommy, who gave me the wagon for Christmas?" I asked, as I settled in next to her by the tree.

"Santa, honey."

After we finished arranging everyone's gifts in their respective areas, my mom stood up and said, "Now we are ready for our company." It was then I remembered my favorite treat at Christmastime.

"Oh Mommy, we *are* going to have peanut butter candy too, right?" I squeaked excitedly.

"Yep, I made plenty," she said as she hugged me tightly.

Our family always gathered together at Christmastime. By midmorning, Uncle Reese and Aunt Maryellen had arrived. My aunt and uncle loved life, and their infectious laughter filled our home with holiday cheer.

Uncle Reese loved to tell the story of the peanuts that sat on a table by his recliner at home. He'd say, "You know, these peanuts used to be covered with Chocolate." We all knew he didn't like peanuts, but he sure loved Chocolate. We all rolled on the floor laughing with the thought that he may have sucked the chocolate off all those peanuts.

Aunt Maryellen was no different. She kept us laughing by finding humor in something as simple as an expression on someone's face. Uncle Reese and Aunt Maryellen have always been two of my favorite people.

After we had a few laughs with them, the showing of the treasures began.

Many Christmases have come and gone since I was a little girl, yet fond memories remain as well as favorite family traditions. Those years have passed quickly, as well as many beloved family members.

Now, my brother and I, along with our children, are entrusted with those special memories and traditions. Can we keep them alive? I hope so.

"Mom, when are we going to Grandmas?" My daughter's question woke me from my Christmas musing.

"Soon, honey."

"Is she making peanut butter candy?"

I hug her tightly, and with a wink and a smile say, "Yes dear, she made plenty."

Mary's Christmas Miracle

Wilma Caraway & Eva Maddox

Oh, Joseph! My husband dear,
Tell me are the angels here.
Surely they are hovering o'er
This babe that millions will adore.

God planned for me to bear this child,
So tiny, perfect, meek, and mild.
Together we will raise God's Son,
And He'll bless the world in days to come.

Oh, Joseph! He's a treasured sight,
How blessed we are this wondrous night!
E'en though this is a lowly place
God has looked on us with favored grace.

He chose a manger filled with hay
On which his newborn Son would lay.
This baby king has no golden crown
But cattle lowing all around.

Oh, Joseph! It's naught that we have done
That God chose us to rear His Son.
No wealth or status can we claim
We're simple vessels to bear His name.

The shepherds heard the angel say
A Savior was born this very day.
They came to see the newborn son
And left rejoicing at what God had done.

Oh, Joseph! Let's pray for God to guide
And give us wisdom whate'er betide.
May we honor God by raising His Son
Who will be the Good News to everyone.

God Bless Us, Every One!

By Peter Mires

The Christmas Season, like other holidays we celebrate, has its share of stories. Many have become so popular that cable television stations show them in 24-hour marathons. When I was growing up—and I just celebrated the big Six-O, so that gives you a context for my formative years—it was the golden age of television. Despite the number of channels that could be counted on the fingers of one hand and that they concluded their broadcast day in the wee hours, I could anticipate with certainty specific holiday movies: *Ben-Hur* every Easter and *A Christmas Carol* every Christmas.

For me, Christmas is intimately associated with the Charles Dickens classic, especially the 1951 version starring Alastair Sim as the miserly curmudgeon Ebenezer Scrooge. My parents, brother, sisters, and I wouldn't dream of missing *A Christmas Carol*; it just wouldn't be Christmas without watching Scrooge embrace the Christmas spirit, albeit only after visitations by the ghosts of Christmas past, present, and yet to come. Oh yes, and his deceased business-partner Jacob Marley played a part in Scrooge's Christmas Eve spiritual metamorphosis. (My brother, in fact, was Marley's ghost in a school play, and

I can still hear him on stage bemoaning, "I wear the chain I forged in life. I made it link by link, and yard by yard.")

As a Christian writer, I've come to appreciate Charles Dickens, the author. I've read and reread *A Christmas Carol*, which at roughly 30,000 words is classified as a novella. With every reading, I discover more of Dickens's literary genius and his spiritual message.

Clearly the most gripping part of the book's plot is the influence of ghosts on the protagonist Scrooge. In fact, the book's subtitle is, "Being a Ghost Story of Christmas." The author doesn't lay claim to this literary device; instead he credits William Shakespeare's *Hamlet*. Dickens writes, "If we were not perfectly convinced that Hamlet's father died before the play began, there would be nothing more remarkable in his taking a stroll at night." This explains his choice for an opening line, "Marley was dead, to begin with."

Dickens was a man with religious conviction and a social conscience. His Christian faith is evident throughout *A Christmas Carol*. He reminds us that besides the feasting and merriment, Christmas is a religious holiday: "But soon the steeples called good people all to church and chapel." That Christmas brings out the child in all of us is also clearly expressed: "For it is good to be children sometimes, and never better than at Christmas, when its mighty Founder was a child himself."

Dickens witnessed the human suffering brought about by England's industrial revolution. He was sensitive to the gulf that existed between the haves and the have-nots, between the prosperous few and masses just eking out a living. In *A Christmas Carol*, these two classes are exemplified by the wealthy Scrooge and his impoverished clerk Bob Cratchit. Dickens was doubtless aware of fellow Englishman

Thomas Malthus's dire prediction of overpopulation (our ability to breed exceeds our ability to feed), evident in Scrooge's words he later regrets, "Are there no prisons? Are there no workhouses?"

The continued popularity of a Dickens novel, such as *Bleak House*, *David Copperfield*, *Great Expectations*, or *A Tale of Two Cities*, is testimony to his ability to tell a wonderful character-driven story. *A Christmas Carol* tops the list of his best known works. It has never been out of print since its publication in 1843.

Although it's a story I turn to every Christmas, its message—the "Christian spirit working kindly in its little sphere"—is worth keeping the whole year round. Scrooge came to personify the Christian spirit. The author writes, "He became as good a friend, as good a master, and as good a man, as the good old city knew, or any other good old city, town, or borough, in the good old world."

Returning to *A Christmas Carol* and my childhood, I related in particular to Bob Cratchit's crippled son Tiny Tim. I had gotten polio in 1955, according to my parents just when I was learning to take my first tentative steps as a bipedal human, and then I couldn't stand or walk. After two operations, lengthy hospital stays, and years of physical therapy, I got my stride back. I'm okay now; I just walk with a little limp. I think it lends distinction to my gate—perhaps a little like Captain Ahab, but that's another story. There was a time, however, when I would be watching *A Christmas Carol* and glance over at my own crutches in the corner of the room. I admired Timothy Cratchit's unwavering faith and continue to delight in his having the final word: "God bless us, every one!"

A Different Christmas Gift

Christine Scott

It was to have been a special Christmas. Our lovely old home was decorated with candles and pine boughs. The aroma of Christmas goodies and pungent pine wafted through the house like a blithe spirit, touching every room.

I had turned sixteen in November and was looking forward to giving my first "boy-girl" Christmas party. I had even convinced Grandmother that we should hang some mistletoe in the front hallway. Grandfather thought that mistletoe was too frivolous and started to protest. Grandmother gave him one of her special looks of mild reproach and amusement, and he was overruled.

Then, just three days before Christmas Eve, the telephone call came. Grandfather answered cheerfully, but his voice soon changed to one of solace. I paused briefly on the stairs waiting to hear what happened. When the call was finished, he turned to Grandmother and said, "Old Mrs. Colmer has passed away." Grandmother put her hand to her mouth, and her eyes were full of pity.

I could only vaguely remember Mrs. Colmer. The Colmer family used to live on a farm next to our extended land. They had a large family, but World War II had disintegrated its unity. The boys went into the service, and the girls went off to the city to make "big" money in the defense plants and other war efforts. Somehow, they never came back to rescue the farm. The farm was sold after Mr. Colmer died. Then, Mrs. Colmer moved into town to live with her remaining daughter in a small apartment.

I hadn't thought of Mrs. Colmer for years. And in that moment, my head was full of candy stripe thoughts of Christmas. Unconcerned, I skipped up the stairs.

Reality came a few minutes later when Grandfather called me to come downstairs. He said solemnly, "There will have to be some preparations made. Members of the Colmer family will have to be our guests until the morning of the twenty fourth."

Before he could continue, I blurted out like a spoiled child, "Oh, that's awful! It will just *ruin* our whole Christmas! How can we have those strangers standing around crying and spoiling our Christmas?"

A sudden icy expression came into Grandfather's eyes, and a blaze of Irish temper flared in Grandmother's glance. Surprised at their anger, I said in a subdued grumble, "Why do they have to stay here ?"

Controlling his anger, he answered, "Because they are a very large family, and the old homestead is gone. They will be coming from different states; some of them will have traveled all night. Neighbors who can take them in are doing so. It is a small effort to make, at a time like this," he finished sadly.

There were no motels in our area of country life. I knew well the rural code of helping out bereaved families. Everyone pitched in, no questions asked. Grandmother began to hustle about putting fresh linens on the guest beds and laying out the warmest quilts. Many arrangements had already been made, and it was decided that one of the Colmer's married daughters would be our guests, along with her husband and a two-year-old child. They would be driving up from Baltimore.

It was nearly eleven o'clock at night when I looked out the upstairs window. The moon had drifted out from the clouds, and the snow had stopped falling. Below my bedroom window, the moonlight's silver splendor had created a giant Christmas card. Suddenly, car lights sliced the quiet picture as a car turned into our long driveway. I watched its tremulous advancement. It skidded and lurched through the rutted pathway toward the house.

I suddenly realized what a hard trip they must have made from Maryland to our mountainous section in Pennsylvania. I knew also that they had gone to the funeral home for the wake and then driven to our house to spend the night. The rumbling car shuddered to a stop. In the dim light from the porch, I saw Grandfather rush out to help lift the sleeping child from the arms of the weary travelers. Grandmother hurried forth to the edge of the porch, ready to give them a supportive hug.

With a lump in my throat and guilt urging me on, I was downstairs in an instant. I was startled to see that they were not much older than myself. And oh, how exhaustion and sorrow had racked their faces. My heart ached for them.

It was a strange thing about that Christmas. I don't remember much about my Christmas Eve party. Nor do I remember if I had kissed a boy under the mistletoe. I do remember that it was a Christmas of giving in a way that I had never given before. I remember, too, that I had not once seen the Colmers cry. But, their faces were swollen with the tears they had shed in the guest room. It was not until years later that I realized how bravely they had tried not to spoil our Christmas with their tears.

Wrapped in my memory will be the vision of the concern and warmth that my grandparents gave to the Colmer family. Yes, it had been a very special Christmas, after all. Never had my home, my family, and my grandparents appeared so precious to me! Still touching the Christmases of my life was the greatest gift of all . . . the gift of appreciation.

From Christine's book, *Vignettes of Small Glories* (Chapter: "Pieces of Rainbows")

Root Beer

Faye Green

❧

I have an old Christmas memory of root beer that creeps into my revelry. It has been a long time since I thought of that story.

I see the small drink bottles with wired glass stoppers to hold the contents under pressure. It must have been months ago when my grandmother made and bottled the root beer. She put it in a cool, dark place. How lucky was my older brother? He could go down to the dark cellar with Dad and help bring the bottles up on this special night. My job was to take the big sugar cookies from the tin and put them, without breaking, on a beautiful glass plate.

Even now, this many years later, I can almost taste the frosty, fizzy deliciousness. I can hear the bubbles rising in the glass and feel the panic that it might bubble over and a precious drop be lost on the kitchen table. I can hear the plop, plop of the ice cubes into the glass and see the bubbles rise again—fast. Sip, slurp, and swoop a taste off the top! Oh, it was as wonderful as I knew it would be.

My brother and I got big round sugar cookies on napkins, tall glasses of my grandmother's homemade root beer, and permission to break the rules and go to the living room with food! At the coffee table, sitting cross legged on the floor, I take a crunchy sweet bite and cold smooth drink. My whole, perfect, wonderful world is illuminated by multicolored bubble lights on our tree. It is heaven.

The first bite and drink leaves me speechless. As soon as the second bite of cookie and second draft of root beer reaches my happy soul, I ask, "Can I have more?" It is childlike and not really selfish. It is my way of pleading to my parents and grandmother for assurance. Can this goodness, this happiness, this joy be sustained?

Children may not understand the desire for joy sustained, but like children, we seek *assurance* that can only come from God. Like children, we turn to our Caretaker and ask—will there be more?

Life is like my Christmas root beer. It may fizz up and spill over. It can deliver temporary pleasure and even invite us to believe in multicolored bubble lights. Those parts of Christmas will not last. But, if we call to our heavenly Father asking for *more*, if we want *heaven*, He smiles on us and says, "Meet my son, Jesus." And then, like sweetness, He gives us the Holy Spirit and there are no rules or limits to where we can take Him—across boundaries to the coffee table, down to the darkest corner, and up to the brightest horizon. Wherever we go, He is there.

Celebrate Christmas

Steve Toney

On holidays we celebrate,
And have ourselves some fun.
But this one is a special time,
To honor God's own Son.

He came to save all sinners,
Who are born upon this Earth.
And that is why this time of year
Brings the wonder of His birth.

He came to die, so we could live.
And He's the Only Way.
And that is why we celebrate,
Each year on Christmas Day.

I know many say, "it's selfishness
And greed that fills our heart."
But why then is it, we see each year,
So many do more than their part,

To touch the lives of people in need,
And those they dearly love,
While laying aside for themselves a treasure,
In their heavenly home above?

No matter what questions people may have,
About why we celebrate: Celebrating is okay.
As long as we know down deep in our hearts,
The love of God is why we have Christmas Day!

Once Upon a Silent Night

Ellen Moore-Banks

Once upon a silent night
The sky was clear, and
The stars shone bright.

A tiny babe laid down to rest
Unaware
That He'd face such tests.

To be nailed to a cross
Between two men
So that one day you and I
Could live again.

One Ugly Caterpillar?

Cheri Fields

I checked my e-mail to see an unusual name. It didn't look like spam, so I opened the message to find it wasn't even really addressed to me. It was a book editor asking for any changes before she sent it on to the printer. It took a while to ponder why she would be passing the message on to me.

Wait a minute, I vaguely remember whipping up a devotional for a Christmas book months ago. Could it be? The next day I noticed an attachment. Scrolling through the index, I saw it: my name in print for the first time.

I couldn't bear to check what I'd written.

Several weeks later, the package with my copy of the book arrived. I showed it to my husband, but didn't want to read more of my words beyond my name. It was still hard to believe.

Finally, with my husband's insistence, I picked it up. To ease the blow, I started at the beginning of the book. Within minutes, I was swept away by the emotions and personalities of the other writers. It was Christmastime, and the story themes were the perfect reminder of why Jesus had come and the difference He makes in the little and big things of life.

Each writer spoke to me in a special way. I was especially delighted by the poetry and the stories of angelic encounters. Many of them started feeling like friends. My only hope standing among these people was the amazing insight God had given me the Christmas before. I clearly remembered what had so struck me and looked forward to seeing His ideas shared with others.

Then I read it, but it was like standing in a spray of machine gun fire. Thoughts came flying at me so fast I didn't have time to take them in. Worst, the point I had most remembered wasn't even clear in the onslaught.

O, Lord, this is embarrassing! Why did they publish me? Why didn't they send it back for major revision? My writing is terrible!

Even as I started thinking these things, His reply came back, *You wrote this less than a year ago. Would you ever send something like this out today?*

Oh, no! I'd never dream of sending something so raw. I can see a bunch of problems instantly.

Keep this book, my dear, echoed through my mind. *It will remind you of how far I've brought you in such a short time. It will help you see what I had to work with when I called you to write.*

Thank you, Lord, I sighed.

But, can I write about what You're showing me to those wonderful people? Otherwise, I'm still going to blush whenever I think about them.

You do that. It will be your own story to add to theirs. I love it when my children see me working in each other. Remember, it's all about Me. Why do you think I let you get away with what you did in the first place?

The warmth of His smile was almost physical. It would be a peaceful and thankful Christmas after all.

The Glo-ori-ori-oria of Christmas!

Sandy Jones

Can you feel it? The air is electric with excitement, anticipation, joy as well as frustration, fear, and anger. Though this is the season to be jolly, we know that some are not. As children of the King, we who belong to Him must be more than "merry" to celebrate this awesome occasion. Even when the world does not understand and so many do not realize what it is they honor at this time, on this day, the symbols of that original gift abound in every detail, from the first appearance of glamorous or gaudy decorations in stores and shops to the quiet and holy candlelit services held on the "Eve."

It excites me more and more every year as I parcel out the things we do to honor the birth of our Risen Lord. First the lights! Every-where there are lights—bright, blinking, white or colorful—yards and streets and buildings, shining with radiant glory. Why have we chosen lights as a first line you might say of holiday cheer? Who is the Light of the World? And He came into the darkness to dispel it; to quench it. For, though darkness may abound, it cannot overcome light; light, however small, destroys darkness. Our King . . . His light has become our light. When you ooh and ahh over the lights, think of that and rejoice heartily that even unaware of what they do, strings of lights are honoring Him.

Silver bells. Can you hear them? Carols playing and, yes, some ridiculous holiday songs as well, but still, there is singing and music. And who gave the first Christmas concert? Angels we have heard on high. There is much to sing about now—the Lord has come. We cannot keep silent. So, another sign of His coming—songs and sounds that remind us of who He is and how He came to be among us.

Commercialism. Oh my, how this stirs some to great disturbance. But think of it this way: shop owners and markets must prepare for the season of gift buying, and if we consider that God was the first gift-giver with unlimited resources, then we should be glad for the variety and availability that they provide for us. God gave His best; when the magi arrived, they brought their best. Instead of feeling negative about the ads and commercials flaunting wares, I choose to appreciate the idea that they keep us in mind of the perfect giver of gifts. It makes shopping much more fun!

All of us have felt the occasional frustration of not knowing what to buy and/or make for someone on our list. Even this can be turned into an act of love when we consider that if we give from our heart, that is the main thing. Once the gift leaves our hands, there is no further responsibility. God gave His best gift and, still, many reject it. This may be part of our "sharing in the sufferings of Christ."

There is also that jolly old guy they call St. Nick, Santa baby, the up-on-the-rooftop guy. Does he not represent our Father in some wild and whimsical way? He brings good things to the children, showers his kind of love upon them with his cheery, cheeky smile and dancing eyes? Does he not share in their excitement by munching on their cookies and milk? And the mysterious fantasy of his reindeer flying sleigh is reminiscent of the angels who appeared to the shepherds, bringing good news of this precious gift called Jesus.

It has long been a puzzle to me about the trees we drag into our homes to load with colorful trinkets and shining baubles. Yes, the history is clearly written, but that is not what I wondered about. Trees and Christmas . . . the tree of life . . . who is life? Jesus.

So, some call it a holiday and think they are avoiding the issue, or they use the X rather than the name of Christ, whose birth we celebrate. What is a holiday but a holy day, and what is the X but the Greek letter for Chi which was used to represent Christ. This practice dates to the sixteenth century from Constantine who converted to Christianity. The chi is written as an X. So Xmas is as much Christmas as the English version we use today.

Perhaps you may not agree with these associations, but to me, history is clear and the Bible says that Jesus is Lord, which is something the world cannot get away from. As it is written, there is nothing new under the sun; indeed there is nothing new under the SON. All that we are, all that we do that is good and positive reflects Him. So, choose the "life" side of Christmas, and enjoy every single moment of this glorious day. And so, have a Hallelujah Christmas everyone! It's a real celebration!

Christmas

Aurie Perkins Shepard Worden

There is no place like Home Sweet Home
When Christmastime comes stealing.
Families and friends all gathered around
A tree up to the ceiling.

There is a gift for everyone
From Grandma to the baby,
All wrapped in paper green and red
And ribbons tied so gaily.

Christmas bells are now ringing
Santa Claus the toys are bringing,
Down the chimney fat Santa goes
Fills the stockings from top to toes.

And on a tray a cake is laid
For Santa Claus that Sissy made.
He ate it all, it was so good,
The way that Sissy knew he would.

Outside the world is white with snow
But Santa knows he has to go,
So up the chimney and over the Plain,
'Til Christmastime returns again.

The Patch Stories

Christine Scott

I finally folded it carefully, packed it in a clear plastic bag and pulled the zipper shut. It was beyond functional use as a bed quilt. The quilt was unbelievably faded and most of its carefully designed patches were hardly recognizable. But, of course, I knew each patch by memory having traced them as a little girl and remembering the stories that went with them.

Actually, my memories of the construction of quilts went all the way back to the image of my grandmother and her sisters. Oh, what a time they had making each and every quilt. They sat for long hours, several on each side of a huge frame which held the heavy material on long rollers. Country women in those days did not drive cars or go out much socially. Hard hours of home making kept them busy and for most of them, quilt making was an acceptable excuse to get together.

There were always wonderful homemade desserts and lots of magpie conversation. As for me, the most exciting part, aside from the gooey desserts, was sitting *under* the quilting table. It formed a perfect tent house for my dolls and me. Once in a while, they would forget that I was under the table and they would shyly begin to talk about some intimate happening. Of course, no sooner were the first few words started, when I would hear a warning gasp from one of them, and they would all peer under the table. Then they would go to great lengths to code their remarks more carefully. Many times I was sent on mysterious errands for lost thimbles or a certain matching yarn which had vaguely been misplaced somewhere.

The quilt that I had wrapped in the storage bag had never been given out as a gift. It had simply been used throughout the family in different bedrooms for many years. When I had been about six years old, I had shared the quilt in my Aunt Evelyn's bedroom. Over and over again, I would beg her to tell me the "Patch Stories."

For almost every patch, which originally came from a huge "scrap bag" of colors, there was a connected memory of the person who had worn the material. My aunt would tell me about her patches that were good memories. She would point to a fragile flowered patch with soft pink and lavender colors and tell me about her first grown-up party dress. Then she would tell about the party and who the boys were and if she liked them and if they liked her.

Black and brown corduroy material made me smile. Those were the days when "knicker pants," which came to the knees, were popular for men. My brother would sometimes receive hand-me-downs and he just hated those old knickers. There was one patch that had little purple sailboats with orange sails; it was a hand me down for me and one of my favorite dresses. Velvet was popular in the quilt patches and a beautiful green one reminded me of Grandmother's special party dress that she cherished so much.

Finally, when I was middle aged, the fading quilt was passed around until it came into my possession. Then I told the stories to my children, but new meanings had become a part of the narration. It seemed to me that the quilt, over the years, had attained a mystical energy of healing powers. No matter how sick one felt or how bad the chills appeared to be, just one wonderful touch of the warm heavy quilt, tucked around the shoulders, sent snuggled contentment. My kids felt its magic and always wanted the old quilt, the minute childhood illness crept into their lives.

Memories of Grandmother tucking the quilt around me was a touch of her love and strength that went beyond cold relief medicine . . . and it certainly surpassed an electric blanket for warmth. There simply was no comparison.

Because I made my home with my paternal grandparents, their children became like older brothers and sisters in their relationships with me. The army and navy colored patches reminded me of my uncles. My uncle Olin had served in the Army. He was a "John Wayne" kind of guy; strong and silent and didn't show sentimental feelings easily. However, when I became very ill with Scarlet Fever, our house had a warning sign placed on the door, which kept us away from the community for thirty days. It was a highly contagious disease and there were no miracle drugs to fight it. So my tall, macho Uncle Olin would sit outside my room, in the upstairs hallway (which was as close as he dared to be) and he would read to me "little girl" stories. He never made fun of them and read them in a way that was delightful to me. It was an unforgettable memory. Later when I was fifteen, he would call me from Johnston to tell me that he named his new baby daughter, Melody Christine, to share my name.

My Uncle Myles could be very sentimental at times and when he was drafted into the Navy, he found himself on distant shores during the Christmas season. He wrote me a letter on censored, old fashioned V-Mail stationery. It was called "Victory Mail" which had to be photographed down to a very small letter. They came in an envelope which had the patriotic colors of red, white, and blue around their borders. We were proud of those letters. And they signified to everyone who saw them, that we had someone special "overseas" who was helping to protect our country. They were read by superiors and photographed for the safety of the soldiers to keep their base destinations as secret as possible.

Much later in time, we would be able to watch our service men and women, right at their duty stations and in battle, by the miracle of television. But the Christmas V-Mail letter, from my Uncle Myles was a highlight moment in my teen years because it told a romantic story.

Alone, and far away from his wife during that Christmas, he wrote to me about the night that he had met her: He had been shopping on Christmas Eve and met a lovely girl, named Edith. Myles had gone to visit friends in Shanksville, and as he entered their living room, he was introduced to four sisters. They were all sitting together on the couch. Their names were Thelma, Ida, Mary, and Edith. As he shook hands with the first three girls, he said, "Hello, I am glad to meet you." However, when he got to the fourth sister, Edith, he said, "Hello, Edith, and I love *you*." And for both of them, it truly was love at first sight. And it was a love that continues through their marriage of sixty years plus.

However, in his letter to me, he wanted to tell me about the Christmas present he was carrying on that special night. Edith was curious and wanted to know who the special gift was for. She was devastated when he replied, "It is for the most wonderful girl in the world!" She thought that he must have a special girlfriend after all. As I read the ending of his letter it contained a lovely message for me:

> *. . . You see, Christine, the gift was for you. Inside the special package was that skating doll that I gave you for Christmas! You were a wonderful little girl. And I hope that you will always stay as sweet as you are.*
> *Your Sailor Uncle*

Once Edith realized her only competition was a little girl, she could fall in love with Myles. And that was a mutual happening on that very special Christmas Eve.

The patches of powder blue and tan were from my Aunt Dorothy's sewing and reminded me of her solidarity and dependability. Dorothy became a no nonsense school teacher and she was loved and admired by many of her students. It was Dorothy who had made the sad trip from Johnstown to Erie, to bring me from the hospital when my mother died during my birth. It was Aunt Dorothy who met my brother, Jimmy Lee, at the Altoona train station, and gave him a tin of her homemade cookies to carry with him. The army was sending him en route to a base in Italy. Feeling already homesick and lost, it was Dorothy, who cheered him on the first leg of a long journey that would take him away from the family for over four years.

As a little girl, when I had shared the quilt with my Aunt Evelyn. I had made her tell me many times about the bright yellow patch. It represented a piece from her costume when she tap danced in the dance review for Gene Kelly's Johnstown Studio. By the time I took possession of the quilt, Gene Kelly had already danced far away from the small lights of Johnstown and had become a shining star in Hollywood. My Grandmother carried the memory of sitting at rehearsals with Gene Kelly's mother, as she followed every move of her talented son. As for Aunt Evelyn, instead of following Gene Kelly's star, she was caught by the ancient message of another star; the star of Bethlehem. Years later, she became a pastor and spent many phases of her life continuing to following that star.

A bold pin stripe patch of black and red had reflected a glimpse of Bob, my own debonair father. He loved artsy colors in vests and ties when they dared to come into vogue, along with the flamboyant era of the 1920's. He would have given anything to have danced to stardom with Gene Kelly, but it was not to be. Outside and away from the steel mills where he worked, the few good clothes that he had, were handsome and immaculate.

And last, but never least in the old fashioned quilt, was the muted gray and brown fabric pieces, from the altered pant cuffs and jackets that belonged to Uncle Joe. He was challenged early in life by the grim reality of Polio; an almost unheard of disease that threatened to spoil his whole life. Years of horrific surgeries and physical struggles could have left him a bitter man. But instead, his gentle, caring spirit was a gift to the whole family. He lived to be almost 90, and managed to make us all forget that he had a physical challenge that he conquered each day of his life.

The patches of the old quilt were like a bond of mystical fabric that somehow wrapped us in the warmth and strength of "family."

We were all uniquely different in personalities, but the threads of endurance, loyalty, and love had woven us together for always.

And in some mysterious way, the fabric of their lives had served to inspire and protect the children and grandchildren that followed in their footsteps. Somewhere in time, I knew that God had fashioned the tapestry of our family, and the victory of *His* creative spirit had touched us all.

From Christine's book, *Vignettes of Small Glories* (Chapter: "Ribbons & Valentines")

The Most Precious Gift

Deborah R. Sullivan

M y desire for you this Christmas
is to bless your precious heart,
with a gift that money cannot purchase
and this poem can be a start.

I want to give you peace and love
and open your heart to joy untold.
I want to see you grow with hope
and watch your faith unfold.

I want to see your expression change
as you realize that God above,
should be the object of your devotion
and is the source of all your love.

I want you to rise above the world
and all its cheap facades.
I want you to relinquish your will
and replace it with your God's.

I want you to know the void man feels,
the loneliness and sorrow,
is because of the hopelessness
men face in a Godless tomorrow.

I want to help you realize
that lives are out of control,
because man has failed to recognize
the Savior of his soul.

God sacrificed His beloved Son,
Jesus was born to die,
to save the souls of desperate men
who are lost and know not why.

Won't you stop to realize
how great His love must be?
Imagine seeing your only son
dying on Calvary.

Man can't know the meaning of love
until he gives it to the Lord.
Then his heart will open to love
each brother in sweet accord.

Because He lives within me,
through His love this Christmas season,
I remind you Christ died for you
and forgave you without reason.

Let Him guide and keep you,
there is so much to gain.
In His Spirit you will reign victorious,
and He will not have died in vain.

The most precious gift this Christmas
you will receive when you know,
Jesus Christ as Savior—
and I profess to you it is so.

Christmas Code Puzzle

Karen H. Whiting

Change each letter to the one before it in the alphabet and each number to the one before it numerically (so replace a 5 with a 4 or a C with a B). Each * is a space between words. It spells out the message the angels told the shepherds on the night Jesus was born. Look up the verse in the Bible to check your answer.

G
PS*
UPEBZ
*JO*UIF*
DJUZ*PG*E
BWJE*B*TBWJ
PS*IBT*CFFO*CP
SO*GPS*CPV*XIP*
JT*NFTTJBI*BOE*MPSE
.*MV
LF*
3:22

Answer Key
(Remember, no peeking
until you have finished the puzzle.)

For today in the city of David a savior has been born for you who is Messiah and Lord (Luke 2:11).

68

Christmas in July

Jean Davis

My sense of grief was heavy after my mother's diagnosis of lung cancer in November 1991. She died the following March. Though I made the trip from Kansas City to southeast Texas to see her three times during that brief period, I had trouble letting my mother go.

That wasn't all I couldn't let go of. The six-foot fragrant cut spruce looked alive when we brought it into the house in mid-December. During my mother's illness, I went through the motions. I felt numb as I put decorations on the tree and did minimal shopping. January came and went. I finally took the lights and ornaments off. February passed. As time slipped by, more and more of the pine needles turned brown and dropped. Finally, I pulled the tree to the back porch, then swept up the wide trail of prickly needles on the floor. My mother was dying. The tree was dying. I couldn't let the tree go.

In July we got a call from my husband's sister, Sara. Her family was moving from Colorado to South Carolina and would like to stop by our house to spend the night if that was okay. Of course it was. My in-laws drove from Texas to Colorado to make the trip with them. My brother-in-law had pancreatic cancer. My father-in-law had prostate cancer that had metastasized to his bones.

I was happy for them to come. Sara's four boys were the same age as our two younger children. It would be good to see them all. But I had a dead Christmas tree on the back porch I needed to do something with.

My mother-in-law, Lois, always said she was happy when we were AUOR—*All Under One Roof.* She looked forward to those times when we could all meet together at their home in Texas. Every meal together at her house was a celebration. Except for my dad and our married daughter and her husband and daughter, we were going to be AUOR for the first time in years.

"What do you want to do with the Christmas tree?" my husband asked.

"Decorate it," I said. How crazy is that, to wrap purple streamers of crepe paper left over from a birthday party around a Charlie Brown tree that now had even fewer of its dead needles after being dragged back through the house into the living room?

When our company arrived, I let them take in the presence of the tree before announcing what we were going to do. Since we were all together, we were going to celebrate Christmas. We drew names. I gave each child and adult a single dollar and a four-for-a-dollar pastel-colored paper bag left over from Easter. Lois, Sara, and I took the children to the nearest dollar store. The men stayed home and assigned someone to buy their gifts for them.

Sara's boys took their assignment seriously. Each present was chosen with care. Each bag was decorated artistically, especially the one with the dinosaur drawing on it. "To" and "From" were written on the bags. I can still remember Sara's laughter when I put the Christmas album on, then the sense of awe I felt when the first album was followed by one of sacred carols. Yes, it was beginning to look a lot like Christmas, and yes, a mighty fortress was our God, a bulwark who had never failed us. The twinkling white lights strung around the room set the mood of wonder. So many memories flooded in of happy times with all our family members present. After we had our traditional Christmas dinner and before we opened gifts, I pulled out my big surprise. Originally from southeast Texas, Kansas snow was a big deal. The previous winter, I had stored some snow in the freezer to make it last. I pulled out my meager supply and sprinkled my guests with it. Oh, what sheer joy!

When we opened our gifts, I got a mirror. My husband's mother got a brush. Jessie got a toy tractor. Libby got a coloring book. The gifts were perfect. Before everyone left the next day, I gave each person a helium-filled balloon and a magic marker. We wrote messages to God, prayers for our loved ones traveling. Then, we let them go. When the van and travel trailer pulled out of our driveway, I wondered if I'd ever see my brother-in-law again.

"What do you want to do with the tree?" my husband asked when we went back into the house. "Want me to drag it to the back porch?" The tree was understandably an embarrassment to our children.

"No." Finally, I was ready to let the tree go.

We had gotten a notice from the trash collection company in December that for disposal, Christmas trees had to be cut into three foot segments and tied in a bundle for pick-up. The bundles needed to be on the curb by the middle of January. When my husband cut and bundled our tree and put it out by the curb in July, I watched from our large living room picture window as the trash truck rattled to a stop in front of our house and the men picked up the tree. I didn't see a single snicker. Maybe we weren't the only family in Kansas City who couldn't let go of their tree in January, either. Later, I got a note from my sister-in-law saying Christmas in July being AUOR was the best Christmas ever. I had to agree. We all needed a few happy memories in the midst of so much heartache.

What I learned that July was this: you don't need to spend a lot of money on Christmas to experience joy. You don't even have to celebrate Christmas on December 25. Christmas is about love and family, about making memories and having fun. For some it's all about being AUOR, sitting around the table with family members enjoying turkey and Grandma's pumpkin pie. For many, it's about hope. The tree can be half dead, or in our case, completely dead. We probably didn't even need a tree. You can use what you have. You can present your gifts in pastel Easter bags. No one will care. You can leave your lights off the tree and decorate with purple streamers instead of Christmas ornaments. It doesn't matter. You can buy your gifts at the dollar store. A Christmas CD and a few children thrown in the mix certainly add to the joy of a heart-warming celebration. And for those without the trimmings of turkey, tree, family or presents, then a grateful heart and awareness of God's presence still makes you rich beyond measure.

Of all our Christmas celebrations, this is the one I remember most. My mother would have loved it, especially the snow. What sustained me through those months and kept Christmas alive, even in July, was the living Christ in my heart.

Harry's Unmentionables

Candy Abbott

I never had a chance to know my mother's father because he died of tuberculosis when she was twelve. But I heard a story about him that I often think of when Christmas rolls around. Now, mind you, I have no idea if the event occurred during the holidays or not, but I have so many wonderful childhood memories of our family Christmases in the northern New Jersey Hoffman home with my cousins, aunts, uncles, and Grandmom, that it seems appropriate to count it as a Christmas story.

If I pause for a moment, even now I can hear the happy hubbub of the adults talking in the living room, the ruckus of my cousin Danny chasing my brothers up and down the wooden staircase, and feel my hand trying to catch a little red ball and scoop up silver jacks as Jane, Helen, Suzy, and Becky sat in a circle with me on the floor, taking turns. I can even smell the mingled aromas of gingerbread men and cinnamon coffee cake, fresh from the oven.

Whether Grandmom corralled her rowdy bunch of grandchildren around her for the sheer fun of it or to protect the breakables in the house—or both—the way I remember it, we were sitting around the kitchen table when she shared her "most embarrassing moment." It didn't take long for my red-faced, perspiring brothers to settle down and begin to hang on her every word. She was quite a storyteller and set the stage by giving us some background. I can see now that she was imparting a legacy of sorts, but at the time, all I wanted was the story.

When Grandmom and Granddad Harry were newlyweds, they lived in a big, stately home. He was a chemist who dressed in a suit and tie and rode the bus into the city where he worked. Grandmom loved being a homemaker, attending to every detail—cooking, cleaning, gardening, and knitting. She even changed the draperies with the seasons and planted sunflowers in the summer that grew so tall they smiled right in the window.

When her most embarrassing moment happened, they hadn't been married very long—just long enough to begin getting irritated with one another every now and then, as healthy couples do. I'll let Grandmom take it from here.

"Your grandfather had a good sense of humor," she told us. "So did I when I was young." A smile spread over her face. "In fact," she said, "I still have a bit of an impish streak of my own, to this very day." She reached over and tickled one grandchild's tummy after another until we were all reduced to giggles.

"You're stalling," I snickered, straightening myself up in the chair. "We want to hear the story. Did you play a practical joke on our grandfather, is that what was embarrassing?"

"You're getting ahead of me," Grandmom winked. "Let's back up to the first time your grandfather left his unmentionables on the floor in the bedroom, right where he took them off. It bothered me, but I didn't say anything, because I wanted to be a good wife."

Jane leaned forward. "Unmentionables?"

"Undergarments. You would call them underclothes or underwear."

"You mean, like his undershirt and underpants?"

Grandmom nodded, and we all giggled.

"But in those days, they were actually called 'unmentionables' because our society was so prim and proper. Even in the privacy of our homes, we were careful about our words and behavior. Things have loosened up a bit in your generation.

"So, what happened next?" Danny asked.

Grandmom smiled. "What happened next is that it became a habit for Harry to leave his unmentionables in a heap on the bedroom floor, and every time I picked up after him, I got a little angrier." She sighed. "One evening, when I got good and tired of it, I held his dirty undies in my hand and shook them at him. 'Harry,' I said, 'you are as able-bodied as I am, and the clothes hamper is only a few feet away from where you're dropping these. Please put them in the hamper from now on.'"

"And did he?" I asked.

"No," she said. "The next night, he made his little pile in the same place. I didn't know if it was intentional or not, but bad habits are hard to break, so I gave him the benefit of the doubt. I reminded him, and he apologized and put them in the hamper. But the next night, he did it again."

"Did you remind him again?" Helen asked.

"Yes, but he had other things to do and never got around to picking them up, so they were still in a heap on the floor when we went to bed."

"So you picked them up in the morning, right?" I said.

"No, I didn't want to become a slave or a nag, so I left them right where they were and never said a word. Besides, by then, we had a little game going. I had established boundaries, and he kept crossing them, but I figured he would come around before he ran out of clean undergarments. I thought that, surely, when he stood in that spot the next night, he would notice on his own and put them in the hamper, but . . . nooo. Guess what he did?"

"What?" we asked in unison.

"He took off that day's underwear and added it to the heap on the floor."

"So the pile of dirty undies got *bigger*," Danny said. By the look in his eye, I could see his mental wheels turning, imagining the pile getting higher and higher and how much fun it would be to jump into it.

Grandmom continued. "That night, and the next night, and the night after that, he did it again. Neither he nor I said a word. We just walked around the pile, day after day, as though it was invisible. I was getting more and more irritated and angrier, until I came up with a most clever idea that took away all my frustrations."

"You jumped in the pile!" Danny grinned.

"No, Danny, that might have been a clever plan for *you*, but remember, I had to do things prim and proper. So I gathered up the whole pile, almost a week's worth of undershirts, socks, and underpants, and took them downstairs to the foyer."

"By the front door?" I asked.

"That's right, honey. And there in the foyer, I got a ladder and carefully hung each piece on the chandelier, like decorating a Christmas tree."

"Ha haaa!" Oh, how we laughed as we visualized that picture she painted for us.

She added, "I felt giddy all afternoon, especially as I fixed dinner, anticipating the moment when Harry would walk through the front door, into our lovely home, and find his unmentionables staring him in the face."

"Tell us, tell us," Helen said. "What did he say when he opened the door?"

Grandmom folded her hands, leaned forward, rested her arms on the table, and looked deep into our eyes before she answered. "He was speechless at first," she said. "He just stood there with his neck craned and his eyes fixed on the extravagant display that dominated the entire room. I was speechless, too. Because his next words were, 'Alice, I'd like you to meet John Grier, the head of our department. I didn't think you'd mind if I brought him home for dinner.'"

It took a minute for us to get it. But when we did, the whole kitchen erupted with laughter!

"So," Jane said, "over dinner you laughed and talked about how your clever idea backfired, right?"

Grandmom shook her head. "I wish we had. But the subject really was 'unmentionable,' so we ate our meal with superficial pleasantries and all did our best to banter about happy things to combat the awkwardness of the scene none of us could get out of our heads. To this day, it remains my most embarrassing moment. And we've had many a good laugh about how we both learned to 'love, honor, and obey' the hard way."

Perpetual Giving

Joyce Sessoms

I grew up in the 60s in a family and community that was monetarily poor, but culturally rich. My mother worked hard to support her four daughters and did an amazing job. I never "felt" poor nor had any thoughts about being less fortunate than anyone else. I was happy.

The year I turned twelve, my mother bought me the bicycle of my dreams. I fell in love with it in the summer of 1963 at the Western Auto store. It was the best Christmas present in the world—a shiny, black English Racer! I was the envy of the neighborhood.

I didn't give a second thought about the sacrifice that my mother had to have made in order to gift me that bike. But I did feel loved and special when I saw it sitting beside the Christmas tree. I can still recall that wonderful feeling fifty years later.

I did not understand the wisdom of what my mother had done until I accepted Christ. He knew the impact that her sacrifice would have on me and that it would cause me to walk in the path that He had already ordained for my life (see Jeremiah 29:11). Christ Himself made the greatest sacrifice of all when He laid down His life so that I might live again (see 1 John 3:16). I thank Him for entrusting me with such an amazing assignment. My professional career and ministry are the same; encouraging youth to discover Him and experience His unconditional, sacrificial love as they seek out the plan that He has for their lives. It is a wonderful gift to understand why you were created and have the opportunity to live it each day.

My English Racer may have been destroyed in a garage fire, but the sacrifice that my mother made for me helped to shape my life. Perhaps unknowingly, she taught me examples of the fruit of the spirit (see Galatians 5:22-23). In the likeness of Christ, she gave me a perpetual gift. One that keeps on giving.

Ring. Ring.

Betty Lewis Kasperski

My friends nicknamed me "Christmas Spirit," aka "CS." Shopping started, decorations were in place, and Christmas carols blasted in the house long before the Halloween candy went on sale. This year found me minus those companions, my bar buddies, for on September 30 at five o'clock I started my sobriety. I passed up "happy hour" at the Coach House and attended a recovery group meeting.

Twenty-five years of having "a drink or two" every day caught up to my body. Test results revealed kidney and liver function numbers out of normal range. These facts confirmed what I could already feel but mentally continued to deny. On top of that, I was aging ahead of schedule, not an avenue I desired to travel.

Mind you, I always functioned well at work—no absenteeism or deadlines missed. But when five o'clock came, I knew where I was headed; husband, children, and dinner could wait. Dave worked in the city with an hour plus commute, two kids were employed out of the area, and Terry played sports, he was never home before six-thirty. This was "my relaxation time," which I felt I deserved, but in reality, my body craved.

A few "brews" or two substantial glasses of wine just took the "edge off," I functioned. No DUI issues, but my day, my life centered around five o'clock and its promise. It was my "freedom," my "independence," or was it?

Nothing earth shattering had happened, no sudden loss, but knowing my alcohol use came before others and myself was its own wake up call. A classic type "A" personality, super achiever, and star player, but underneath, I knew I was one drink away from losing every-thing. It was in charge of my life, not me. Indeed, a sobering thought.

My bar friends called a couple of times to ask why I wasn't there. When I told them I was in a recovery program, the response was si-lence or a quiet, "Oh." What we had in common, drinking, now was subtracted from the equation. The call ended awkwardly and quickly; our bond was severed. Almost like they didn't want to catch what I had or deal with what they embraced. Probably others in their lives wanted them to take the step I had. They didn't need one more person calling them to that path.

The word got around and the calls stopped. What also surprised me was that I actually know very little about my bar buddies—the five o'clock club, except first names. What an irony, I thought, since groups where you share and hear everything, only use first names.

As Christmas got closer, I longed for the camaraderie of my old friends. Maybe I could just go this Friday and have seltzer with lemon—no wine—and enjoy a few laughs. My sponsor quickly nixed that idea. "You are a babe in recovery; you don't jump into the deep end of the pool." I listened albeit reluctantly.

As I was considering my weekend social options, my cell phone rang.

"Hey, Sallie, how are you? It's Vivian from church."

"Good. What's up?"

"I just got a call from Audrey; she coordinates the schedule for the folks from our church who ring bells for the Salvation Army at Chambers department store. One of the volunteers took ill and cannot be there tomorrow from noon until two. Would you be willing to help us out?"

A silent pause at my end, while I searched for a reason to say, "No."

"There would be another person with you, and the station is just inside the main doors. Weather is not an issue." Vivian said.

"I've never done this before. What is involved?"

"Just ring the bell, smile, and wish people a Merry Christmas. Oh, and you can wear a Santa hat if you like."

"No handing out tracts?"

"No."

"Okay, I'll do it." I said running out of excuses.

"Thanks, Sallie, just be there fifteen minutes before your shift. God bless."

What had I just volunteered for? I'm a quiet person by nature, not a bell ringing solicitor. Well, two hours is manageable. I'll mirror the other person. One time won't kill me. I'll go shopping after my shift.

At dinner I didn't even share with Dave and Terry what I would be doing, just that I was going to Chambers to do some Christmas shopping. As long as they were not expected to come along, no questions came my way.

I opted to don a simple red and white Mrs. Claus hat and arrived at the store before noon relieving the other shift.

"Hi, I'm Charlie. You must be Sallie, glad you were able to come," as he displayed a warm smile.

"I don't know what to do; it is my first experience as a bell ringer."

"It's easy. I've been doing this for twelve years. It wouldn't be Christmas for me without this ministry."

"Ministry?"

"Yes, because what we collect helps so many people."

"But it's just loose change or a dollar or two." I said.

"You'll see. Here's your bell."

Ring. Ring.

"Good afternoon." Charlie called to two passersby. They nodded and kept going.

Ring. Ring.

"Good afternoon." I called to a young mother with two children in tow. She did not respond, too focused on gripping their little hands.

Ring. Ring.

"Good afternoon." Clink. Clink. "Thank you, Merry Christmas." Charlie responded.

"Merry Christmas to you. Thank you." She called as she rushed into the store.

Ring. Ring.

My bell called, but another couple looked away and moved quickly into the store, discarding my request.

Ring. Ring.

"Good afternoon." Charlie said.

Getting a bit exasperated I said to him, "Doesn't it bother you when people make a point of ignoring you?"

"No, not everyone can give or will give. It's okay."

"Don't you feel like you are begging?" I asked.

"No, only asking for their help, just keep ringing."

My type "A" personality, expecting quick results, was not happy. I checked my watch, an hour and forty minutes to go. Don't think I have the "Pied Piper" gene.

Ring. Ring.

Clink. Clink.

"Thank you, Merry Christmas," I said.

"Merry Christmas, Sallie, nice to see you. See you Tuesday," she said.

I didn't make the connection at first; she was "out of context." Where did I know her from?

She noticed my confusion. "It's Amy. I'm an . . ." I knew the missing word, alcoholic.

"Yes, see you Tuesday, at noon," I answered.

Ring. Ring.

"Thank you, Merry Christmas." Charlie smiled as a large bill landed in the bucket.

Ring. Ring.

Sharing this fact was embarrassing, but I wanted to score a big donation, a charity "big hit" for a good cause, of course.

Ring. Ring. Ring.

I gestured with newfound enthusiasm. A young boy holding his father's hand stopped at the bucket and reached down into his pocket and came up with a nickel and a dime. An almost inaudible "clink, clink" sounded as the coins dropped in.

"Thank you. Merry Christmas," I said.

"Merry Christmas," the little voice called. "I hope that helps another boy or girl."

"I'm sure it will," I said, feeling a lump swelling in my throat.

I watched as he skipped beside his dad into the store, happy with what he had done for someone else. *Out of the mouths of babes,* I thought. *Drop your "I have to have the biggest donation" attitude.* This child righted my Christmas spirit. Give from the heart for others. The rest of my shift flew by. The donations may not have been huge, but the message I learned was gigantic.

That day was the beginning of many shifts ringing the bell. It was a ministry of helping others. But the biggest gift came my way, I traded "happy hour" for a bell of joy.

Ring. Ring.

Merry Christmas!

The Piece-able Kingdom

Kathryn Newman Schongar

No other time than Christmas
Do we get the table out
And spread a thousand jigsaw
Puzzle pieces all about.

Then as we turn each right side up
The first through to the last,
The season's silent calm compels
Reflection on the past.

I think your world's a puzzle, Lord.
We know how it should look;
You had Isaiah prophesy
That view within his book:

"The lion lies beside the lamb
In peace," is what one reads.
And just as strange, the Bible says,
"It'll be a child who leads."

Lord, I believe we're each a piece
That has a job to do,
No matter what our size or shape,
Location, or our hue.

Each may not be a corner piece
Or central to the scene,
Yet, each can be a reaching link
That's needed in between.

Please place your pieces right side up
And help each find its site
By sending forth the Christmas Child's
Illuminating light.

It's Not Time Yet

L. Claire Smith

I watched my aunt stand at the window, a cup of steaming tea in her hand. She sipped delicately, watching a pair of cardinals at the bird feeder.

"Bird watching?" I asked.

She nodded. "The cardinals. Such a brilliant red."

"They're beautiful, but so are all the others."

"They are," she agreed equitably. "But I have a soft spot for cardinals."

"And that is because . . ."

"A cardinal saved my life once."

"Oh, come now, a little bitty bird like that? How could it save your life?"

"Just by being what it is and doing what it does."

"Would you explain, Aunt?" I asked.

"Surely. It happened a long, long time ago, but my encounter with the cardinal changed my life. Reaching into her bag, she brought out a notebook and placed it before me. I've been recording that very memory," she said. "I hope you will find it meaningful."

"I was angry; my emotions were seething, my mind spouting bitter scalding thoughts, my will resentful. I was in complete rejection. I felt betrayed, abandoned, left high and dry, marooned in a place where I was misunderstood and unwanted. And I had had enough.

"The place where I had been shipped off to was near a river. I wasn't sure how far away the river was, but I was sure I could get to it, and when I did, I would end it all. I was tired of trying to fit in, trying to please everyone, trying to match everyone else's idea of what I should be. I had no idea who I really was, but I certainly wasn't what others thought I should be. I didn't fit anyone's mold, and why should I? I had just as much right to be myself as anyone else, but when I tried to be *me*, when I tried to find out what and who I was and act accordingly, I got smashed down by others who were cruel and unsympathetic. Well, enough. I was through.

"To reach the river I had to walk down a hill to the wide valley floor. I berated myself as I trudged along. *You're a fool,* I told myself. *Anyone with half a functioning brain who has been through what you have experienced would know that you can't trust people. You'd think you'd learn, but you never do. Time and again you follow the advice of someone you think has your best interest at heart, and time and again you get slapped up beside the head. Talk about stupid! Well, this is the last time. I'm through! The world can take the advice of all these 'well-meaning' people and stick it. Nobody really cares about me. I refuse to be somebody's experimental plaything. I'm better off dead, and I'll make sure that happens.*

"The bleak northern winter landscape lay all around me the desolateness surpassed by the bleakness in my soul. According to what I had been taught, God probably wasn't too happy with my thoughts or intentions. Too bad, I thought. God can just get over it. I glanced at the leaden grey sky. It looked like snow would be upon us soon. Too bad, I thought again. In a couple of hours the weather won't matter ever again.

"Suddenly, across that desolate, dreary landscape darted a streak of brilliant red. My attention caught, I watched as a cardinal headed for the topmost branch of the tallest tree. All is not lost, his presence seemed to say. Somewhere down in the lowest level of my heart a flicker of hope responded to that streak of scarlet. He hung there getting his balance. Then, a few seconds later, the air was filled with the sound of his song. Liquid joy poured from his throat, cutting through the surrounding desolation with a promise."

"'Cheer up; cheer up. All is not lost,' he seemed to say, his declaration somehow soothing.

"I leaned against the trunk of a tree watching this one dab of color defy the hopelessness of the dead and dying season. As I did so I heard another sound, the small sound of running water.

"Water running in the wintertime? Was I closer to the river than I thought? I frowned and looked down at my feet. I found not the river, but a spring. This was something new. The springs I knew about all froze during the winter, keeping their laughing voices locked until spring turned them loose. Yet here was one, nestled in a tiny basin among the roots of three close-growing trees, bubbling merrily in the cold of January.

"As I studied that spring, the lesson fell into my mind complete:

"Foundation: The spring was the surface of a greater body of underground water deep and powerful enough to push the water upward. As long as the underground body of water continued, as long as nothing got in the way of the connecting channel, the spring would always have water no matter what the surface conditions looked like. As long as the spring continued to push its contents outward, the water would remain fresh. Living entities without the benefit of movement would draw their needed sustenance from the living, moving water. Entities capable of movement would come to drink at the life-giving water whenever in need.

"Challenges: I saw stones at the bottom of the spring's basin. They were rounded, polished and shaped by the continuous flow of the water. Had they always been so or had they once been angular and sharp? Did those sharp edges 'hurt' the water as it flowed over them? Had the water chosen to continue its work no matter what the difficulty or the cost to itself?

"Obstacles: The roots of the surrounding trees helped form the spring's origin basin. What would happen if the spring refused to break over the barriers, content to stay within the confines defined by the tree roots? The basin would become a stagnant pool, the water no longer fresh but a container of undesirable growth, becoming a home for decay and even death. Because of the unhealthy aspects of the water, entities with movement would no longer frequent the spring. They would move away, finding another healthy source of water. Those entities without benefit of movement would die, the life-force being crowded out by the undesirable growth.

"Breakthrough: If the spring refused to let the encircling roots confine its waters, calling upon its source for help, it would find a way over the barrier, forming a tiny waterfall, establish-

ing its own little stream. That tiny waterfall would give the spring a happy voice, spreading the sound of merriment at the overcoming of whatever barricaded its way.

"I stood silent as the lesson lay before me. The application was easy to understand. 'You want me to go back, don't You?' I whispered in despair.

"*Yes.*

"I leaned against the tree and finally let the tears come. I sobbed out my sorrow, the wind turning my tears to ice crystals.

"I don't want to go back. They don't want me there.

"*I know. You are different, and they don't know what to do with you.*

"They don't like me. I'm trying to be myself, whatever that looks like. I have no intention of hurting them.

"*I created you to be unique. You don't fit into any of their categories. They are afraid of you, and their fear makes them angry. They don't know how to think outside of the box, and they have the tendency to try to destroy what they fear.*

"Can't I just come home to You?

"*No, child.*

"Why not? Don't You want me either?

"*I do want you, and one day you will join me, but it's not time yet. I want you to go back, to learn what you can while you're here, to grow and mature. I am making you into a special vessel for My use. Those others will help Me do that. You have begun to learn one of the most painful, yet valuable lessons people can learn.*

"Which is?

"People are never enough. A relationship with Me is the only way to be fully satisfied. I promise that one day you will look back and see that what I wrote in Romans 8:28 is really true. All things do work for good to those who love Me. Be assured, My child, even when you stumble in the dark, you are never alone. I have started you on this journey, and I will never leave you by yourself. Call on Me, and I will answer. The cardinal and the spring will help to comfort you.

"Still grieving I dried my tears on the back of my mittens, turned, and trudged back up the hill, across the road, and onto the campus, resigned to learn what I could among a group of people to whom I was like an alien.

"The road has been long and often painful. To this day, the flight of a cardinal or the glimpse of a spring reminds me to hope. And He was right. I can look back and agree that all things work together for good to those who love God."

Missing Faces Round the Christmas Tree

Kristin Whitaker

We're missing several faces, Lord,
'Round the Christmas tree this year.
But thank you for sweet memories
Of those we still hold dear.

Though none of us could ever take
Their place in any way,
Please, help us share their blessings
With others sent this way.

May each remembered kindness
Inspire us to do more,
And every traveler join us
On the road to Heaven's door.

We know You love and guide us,
But broken still, we kneel
And lift our hearts to You, Lord—
Please, show us how to heal.

And next year when we gather,
May memories sweeter be,
Our sorrows healed and fading
Into Your eternity.

Home for Christmas

Wilma S. Caraway

"*Sprechen sie Deutsch? Ja? Nein?*" Elton asked as he perched on a stool near the counter where I had just placed a dish of chocolate chip cookies.

"Do I speak German? Are you crazy? No! *Nein! Nein! Nein!*"

"And why do you ask, Mr. Caraway?"

"Well, Mrs. Caraway," he said, as he munched on a warm cookie. "Remember that job I applied for with Central Texas College?"

"Sure, I remember very well. Are you trying to tell me something?"

"I sure am. I got the job. I will be the automotive department chairperson. I will set up classes for overseas military personnel. Isn't that exciting? But the bad news . . ."

"Wait a minute. You come in and tell me good news and then you spring bad news on me. Which is it, good or bad?"

"Well, the bad news is that we don't have much time. I know how you love Christmas."

"Don't tell me we have to be there before Christmas."

"Like I said, I know how you love Christmas with all the hustle and bustle. But we do need to be there soon after Christmas."

"What? Christmas is less than three months away. And we have to move after Christmas?"

No more cookies for you, Mister!

"You will still get to do the shopping, tree trimming, and baking."

"But what about my job, the house, the *KIDS?*"

"We can do this," Elton said. He grabbed a handful of cookies and a glass of milk and added, "Let's put a pencil to it."

I got a tablet and pen. We sat at the table and began our "To Do List." *This is going to be exciting but challenging.*

First, tell the kids. We realized that it wasn't going to be easy to convince Jenna and Gerald that a move like this is an opportunity of a lifetime. They would be leaving their friends and not to mention a menagerie of pets. We would need to find homes for the dog, two rabbits, a donkey and two squirrel monkeys. The monkeys were acquired when the kids were reading the pet section of the Sunday paper one day. Then, we have to get passports. But with all that was on the list, what concerned me the most was that we have to sell the house. It wasn't ready to sell. There were repairs to be made and paint to be touched up. With everything we had to do and with Christmas just around the corner, it seemed impossible. *Oh ye of little faith.*

It wasn't too long after that cookie and milk meeting with Elton that our "to do list" was becoming our "all done list." The animals had new homes, and the kids were starting to get a little excited about living in another country. But I was still worried about the house. We had finished the repairs and the painting touch ups. And our time clock was ticking down.

I didn't see how we could sell the house before we left for Germany. It was Christmastime, and people do not buy houses at Christmas. Oh well, maybe we could rent it. With no solution in sight, I decided I would go to the PTA meeting. I have always been active in my kids' schools, rarely missing a PTA meeting, but for some reason, I could not get out of the house that night. Finally, I was ready to leave and the phone rang.

"Mrs. Caraway, I know it is late, but my husband and I would like to come see your house tonight."

Really, this late? I could say no. But this was the *first* call on the house we had received. I tided up before the couple arrived. As they walked through the house, I could see they were interested, but did not expect to hear them say. "I think we will take it."

"Excuse me, what did you say?"

"We will take it."

The to do list was now done. *Thank You, Lord. Thank You, Lord.*

Before leaving the house for the last time and pulling the door closed behind me, I gazed around the living room and my eyes pooled as I recalled memories past of twinkling lights on our tall Christmas tree and presents beneath. I couldn't believe we would not be home for Christmas.

We said goodbye to our wonderful friends and our loving church family. We enjoyed a bittersweet Christmas with our parents and other family members before departing for Germany.

We arrived in Winzenheim, our new home, in January. We busied ourselves with learning the German language and culture, visiting many historic sites, magnificent castles, and tourist attractions. The months passed in a blur, and it didn't seem possible to me that it was Christmas again. We visited the famous Kris Kindle Mart in Nuremburg where I purchased candles for our Christmas tree.

A Christmas party hosted by the Central Texas College-Overseas administrators was held for the faculty, staff, and their families in the quaint Ronneberg Castle. Yes, a real castle and I felt like Cinderella in my formal gown. We drove through small villages on narrow winding roads and up the snow-covered mountain to the castle. Inside the castle door, we stood in awe as we glanced around the room. There was a *hugh* Christmas tree decorated with tinsel, shining ornaments, and colored Christmas lights. The tables were covered with red cloths and a centerpiece of pinecones, greenery, and red candles. The aroma wafting from the kitchen added to the warmth and friendship we shared. We enjoyed visiting with our CTC family and eating the fantastic German cuisine. We sang Christmas carols and concluded with *O Tannembaum—O Christmas Tree* before the benediction. Then as we were saying our goodbyes and wishing everyone a *Frohliche Weihnachten–Merry Christmas,* we noticed it had begun to snow. What a wonderful scene watching the softly falling snowflakes shimmering in the outdoor lights of the ancient castle.

On our drive home, we saw magical and fantastic sights. We were amazed as we glanced around at the twinkling Christmas lights, the colorful decorations, and the beautiful falling snowflakes glistening in the streetlights. Upon arriving home, we gathered in the living room where I carefully lit each candle on the tree. We enjoyed watching the glow and flickering of the candle flames as we sang *Silent Night* and thanked God for our new home and new friends.

Home . . . I love the sound of that word, and we *were* home for Christmas.

I thought about the irony that Jesus, whose birthday we celebrate, had no place to call home while on earth. But today, He *is* home for Christmas!

Once Upon a Christmas

Christine Scott

Although many deeply religious people do not acknowledge Santa Claus as a part of Christmas, we have been continuously bombarded with its magical effect throughout the years. It continues to be merged within our culture and captures a certain delight within the young and the very old . . . and those of us in between. Nearly every child, in their "heart of hearts," has dreamed of the wonder of Santa Claus.

I was about five years old when the mystery of Santa Claus began to plague my every waking moment. Was he for *real*? Did he *really* have a sleigh? And what about those mysterious *reindeer*? By Christmas Eve, I was frantic for proof of his existence—for REAL! So, on this very special Christmas Eve, I was put to bed at an unthinkable early hour. I just thought and thought about good ole' Santa. But my weary little head couldn't seem to find the answers to all my questions.

I was in a huge old bed with a "Granny Quilt" pulled up to my chin. Peering over the mound of covers, I could see the bedroom window. A huge, white winter moon shimmered in the night sky. Did the moon have a face? Of course he did when seen by my wide-awake eyes. And I kept my glance riveted on his face. Then, it happened—to the left of the moon, several tiny specks emerged.

To my astonishment, I realized the specks had become reindeer! They were so far, far up in the sky that they had only tiny bodies. But they were reindeer, *for sure.* Within seconds, it was an unforgettable scene as the miniature sleigh followed the reindeer. Without a doubt, I could glimpse a SANTA at the reins! They just glided slowly and beautifully right across the smiling face of the moon! I wanted to shout and perhaps run to the window, but pure enchantment tingled through my body. I didn't dare move, and not a sound came from my lips. In a few unforgettable minutes, the lovely sight disappeared into a field of sparkling stars. But I knew that every detail would be cherished forever in my memory. I was out of bed in a flash and headed for the stairs.

I reached the banister at the top of the steps and stopped abruptly. I heard laughter and voices below. Peeking carefully through the banister rails, I surveyed the living room. There were quite a few adults gathered around the Christmas Tree. But only one figure stood out vividly, Santa Claus!

He was putting a new red tricycle under the tree. It was MY tricycle! My heart pounded. I wanted to dash down the stairs. But something stopped me; the golden image of the Santa sleigh riding across the moon. I knew then that I had witnessed a HUGE secret. I knew that I must keep that secret all to myself or the magic would disappear. Silently, I crept back to the old-fashioned bed to dream the best of sugar plum dreams.

The next morning, it was all for real. There stood the tricycle! I could keep the secret not a second longer, and I blurted out the whole story of Santa on the moon. The family exchanged "knowing glances" and chuckles of amusement. Had a neighbor been dressed in a Santa Claus suit and placed the bike? Had I really SEEN him do that? And what about the Santa on the moon?

Fortunately, I will never know the facts from fiction concerning that wonderful night. But what I do know is that, years later, when my own children asked about Santa Claus, the magic burst forth again. And it glowed from my eyes to theirs in one simple heartbeat.

From Christine's book, *Vignettes of Small Glories* (Chapter: "Circles & Glories")

The Christmas Spirit at Heart

Rita Schrider

Christmas can be a time of despair
Listen to me, all who dare.

The Christmas magic is full of faith
The kind that some people choose to hate.

The meaning of Christmas is found through all sorts of reason
But it is the birth of Christ that is the true season.

We anticipate the magic of Christmas, to share and to please
Oh, how we dread the financial burden the season does leave.

We count down the days until the magic is seen
But what kind of magic do we dare to dream?

Every year, I look back at the ones before,
And I vow it will be different; but how, if I want more?

I start off knowing the true Christmas spirit
At heart, believing that Christ is the one true part.

Over time, we fall into the demands of the bustle of the season,
Quickly losing the light of the reason.

I know in my heart that Christ is the reason,
How can I keep it through all the season?

I think I will try and keep the spirit alive by loving God's Word,
It is the one thing we just can't deny,

I need to hold fast to the love that He gives me;
I can wrap it in the gifts that I lay under my tree.

Oh, how will I find the love that Christmas is meant to be?
If I only hold on to it and get down on my knees!

Please, Lord, fill me with your peace this Christmas season.
Let me remember the price of the reason.

Christmas Eve Critter Mysteries

Anna Buckler

To Stun a Mockingbird

David and I both heard it. What? A hard thump came from our bedroom window. We looked to see what it could be. You guessed it. A mockingbird. At first glance, we were sure he was dead, but then he fluttered his wings a little. Aha! He's not dead but managed to knock himself out. What to do? We started praying with our final request to God, his Creator, that he would fly again. I got a brain wave of a thought; *I'll anoint Mr. Bird!* But how? The poor thing might die of cardiac arrest if I do. Well, I sneaked up on him from behind on all fours, inching my way closer and closer. Aha! The tail feathers were within my reach. I anointed him with a drop of oil. Mission accomplished.

We went to church for the Christmas Eve service. When we returned, Mr. Bird was gone. I was so happy! But David said a predator got him. *Where's his faith?*

The next day Mr. Bird wasn't in his usual tree, so I began to think there might be trouble, after all. But when I went out our back door, there he was, heralding me as usual.

I truly believe God answered our prayers for that little fellow. Mr. Bird is definitely flying again this Christmas Day!

Flying African Clown Knife

We had a 55-gallon aquarium loaded with all kinds of fish, one of which was the African Clown Knife. He was large for a clown fish, about four inches long and solid gray with large black circles on his belly.

Another Christmas Eve, around 2 a.m., I awoke to a thump, thump, thump noise. I couldn't tell exactly where it was coming from. I investigated the closed-off rooms, thinking it was our cat romping around somewhere. Nope, the noise wasn't the cat. By this time, I heard the thump, thump, thump again, coming from the living room. For some reason, I didn't turn on any lights. I narrowed the noise down as coming from underneath the sofa. I ran my hands under the sofa to find a somewhat dried up fish. I gently lifted him and put him back into the aquarium.

On Christmas morning, I checked him and found he had a few scrapes and quite a bit of carpet lint in the tank. We believe the African Clown Knife fish misjudged his own strength in his daily dive, always to the top of the lid. He must have "flown" through the air about three feet to land underneath the sofa. Normally a sound sleeper, it is a marvel to me that I was awakened. I praise God too that the fish was noisy and kept it up!

I'm convinced *all* creatures are important to God, especially at Christmas, a season of miracles.

Tree of Joy, Tree of Love

Wilma S. Caraway

JOY
LOVE
FAITH
BELIEF
RESPECT
PATIENCE
REVERENCE
GENTLENESS
HELPFULNESS
FAITHFULNESS
UNDERSTANDING
ENCOURAGEMENT
TRIMMED
WITH
LOVE

A Christmas to Remember

Eva Maddox

"No gifts this year!"

"Mo-om!" Sherry said, her hands on her hips as frustration wrinkled her forehead.

"No gifts that you wrap, that is."

I took note of my son, Rod, who rolled his eyes at Kristi. I knew what they were thinking. *There goes Mom again with one of her crazy ideas.*

Guilty as charged. I have been known to plan some pretty creative Christmas activities at our annual gathering.

"We're each going to bring a special dish that we make."

"Can't we just buy something?" Danny asked.

"Nope! Something you *make*."

"Well, that's not so bad," Kristi said.

"I'm not finished, yet."

Groans all around.

"We each have to *do* something."

"What does *that* mean?" Sherry asked.

"Well, all four of you can play an instrument. You can sing and you can write, too. So, your gift to the family is sharing a song, a poem, a reading or some other creative gift that is specifically from you.

I waited for their reactions. Whether it was the fact that they didn't have to spend money on gifts or if they genuinely liked the idea, they didn't balk.

Because we had no family living near us, we always invited two or three other families to join us for our Christmas get-together. I passed the word about our "creative Christmas" plans to those we invited, and all happily agreed to participate.

In 1984, Christmas Eve blew in with a snow storm amid its usual magic of twinkling lights and soft carols. Guests arrived dressed in their red Christmas sweaters, sweat shirts, ties, and dresses. Each carried a dish. I chuckled at the look of pride on their faces. *So far, looks like my idea is working.*

All sixteen of us held hands as our friend, Tom, said grace.

Before feasting, each person shared the name of the dish they brought. Amazingly, there were no duplicates. My son, Danny, single-handedly made a French silk pie. Yum!

We jammed into the living room and launched into our "gift giving."

There were solos, duets, a piano piece, a flute number, poems and a reading. It was fun, punctuated with laughter, and most of all, meaningful. Rod read the Christmas story found in Luke, and *Silent Night* closed a perfect evening.

In the hustle and bustle of the Christmas season, we tend to forget the *reason* for Christmas. That evening, twenty-nine years ago, the name of Jesus was exalted through word and song. I like to think it pleased the Lord Jesus.

While we didn't repeat that idea, we never failed to remember that it is the birthday of our Savior that we celebrate on December 25.

Christmas Cannot Be Christmas

Mary Emma Tisinger

W ithout love.

Without someone to love
and to be loved by.

Without a child to hold,
and wonder
at the wonder in his eyes.

Without a song in the air,
or a star shining bright
atop the Christmas tree,
like the star in the sky
that the wise men followed,
bearing gifts for a king.

Without the Christmas story
of angels,
and shepherds
keeping watch at night.

Without Mary and Joseph
in a stable in Bethlehem,
and a baby born . . .

the Christ child,
God with us,
Jesus.

Christmas morn.

My Most Memorable Christmas Gift

Sue Segar

It was Christmas 1990, two years after my husband's grandmother died. We purchased the house from her estate three months earlier. And so, every weekend, we traveled an hour and a half each way from our two-bedroom condo in the suburbs of Baltimore to our "new" home on Maryland's Eastern Shore.

The house hadn't been lived in regularly for over a decade. The walls told of a lifetime of activity, smoking being one of them. We'd spent every weekend since purchasing the five-bedroom monstrosity cleaning. I remember saying I didn't want to move in until it was scrubbed, at least the most used areas in which we would live.

We decided that since we spent no free time together at the condo, we would forego a Christmas tree that year. My husband knew that Christmas was my favorite holiday. He also knew I had already planned to get a tree the next year and place it in the bay window of the big old place. I had envisioned that from the first day, I realized we would actually own the house. He knew the color scheme I had chosen and that I insisted the tree would have white lights to look like snow.

Growing up, I enjoyed colored lights. Maybe I should say, my dad enjoyed decorating with colored lights to see the joy on our faces when he turned on the switch. My husband's family wasn't accustomed to having any lights at all. I knew that the compromise would be pleasing to both families.

The Christmas season was upon us. We were making the trip to the Shore to celebrate Christmas with my husband's family. We weren't certain if we would spend any of our weekend working at the house. My husband was adamant about stopping by and checking on something there. I insisted that whatever it was, it could be done the next day.

My head was bobbing, I was exhausted from my work week and it was so late, it was actually early. One a.m. to be exact. It was also particularly cold.

Why does he want to check on the house NOW? I am sure it won't change any if we wait until daylight! Ugh! I whined to myself after he got out.

I was thankful that he told me, "Wait in the car, I'll just be a minute."

My head sank as I nodded off toward sleep. Suddenly, I was startled awake by the luminous glow of the entire bay window side of the house, and I was reminded just how much my husband really did love me. I jumped out of the car and catapulted myself into our new home.

The majestic scene will be forever ingrained in my memory: the room with its six windows, three of which make up the bay, with curtains open, and the pine wood floor that held over a century of wear. The nine-foot ceiling which had recently become white as snow made the ambiance of the room more magnificent. There was nothing else in the massive room, no furniture whatsoever, just the two of us and the beautiful tree, the best Christmas gift ever.

We went together to unplug the lights. I remember the majestic feeling that overwhelmed me, pure joy as my husband of a mere four years described how he and his mother got together during the week to purchase the tree and needed accessories and how they lovingly decorated it. It brings tears to my eyes to this day, 20-plus years later. Since then, I have experienced an even greater Christmas gift. I have come to know Christ as my personal Savior, and in Him, I rest all of my cares. As I relive my experience with my most memorable Christmas gift, I am reminded of how magnificent our God is. He loves us so much, He was willing to give us the best gift of all, eternal life in Christ Jesus.

A Child Came

Michele Jones

A child came quietly in the night
Wrapped in swaddling cloth He lay
In a manger filled with hay
As the stars shone brightly above
Now here upon the earth
The Incarnate Son
Fulfillment of God's continuous love

To bring us restoration
Reuniting us to Him through Christ
While angels' proclamations
Resound throughout the night
Good news and great joy
For all generations
This is the Christ child
Who has been sent to save us

He came in all humility
No pomp or parade
His mission alone
Mankind He would save

His birth would have no meaning
Were it not for the cross
Where He chose to lay down His life
To ensure not all are lost
Our greatest celebration
Is that He rose up from the grave
Death has been defeated
We are no longer captive as sin's slave
We have been set free
Our sins have been erased

All because a child
Came quietly in the night
Changing the world forever
On that mostly holy of nights

A 1960s Christmas

Kathleen Talbott

"Mom, the mailman is here!" I ran to the mailbox, and the postman winked at me as he opened the lid. I saw the brown paper wrapper and knew exactly what it was as I pulled it out of the mailbox. For verification, I poked my finger under the wrapper to feel the smooth, expensive paper and peeked at the cover. I would be the first to see it.

The arrival of the Sear's Christmas catalog heralded that Christmas preparations would begin. That meant my siblings—Mike, David, Roni—and I were about to begin fighting over it, so we could decide what we wanted from Santa. Mary Ellen was almost a year old so she didn't get into the ruckus until a few years later. Julie wouldn't be born for another five years.

Our parents told us that we needed to make our list of toys and they would tell Santa. He would bring us toys if we were good, of course! Most of the time, the toys were not exactly what we saw in the catalog so that would validate that Santa brought them, not Mom and Dad.

"Kids, come here," Mom called from the kitchen.

Once we were sitting at the kitchen table, she continued. "The Christmas catalog is here."

"Yea!" we all shouted.

"I get it first." David, who was usually quiet, spoke up first quickly.

"Now, I don't want any fighting over it this year. Each of you will get thirty minutes on school nights to look at it to decide what you want."

"Ah, Mom, that's not enough time," Mike said mournfully.

"Yeah, Mom, it's not," David chimed in.

"Yes, it is. Remember, you each have $25 to spend."

Roni and I were quiet. I had already spent most of the day perusing the catalog and reluctantly shared it with Roni when she came home from school. We were content for a while.

Even though Mom had high hopes, eventually her chores kept her away from timing us. We all improvised, and the bickering started. Thankfully, for our parents' sake, my brothers were quick to decide. It was finally given to Roni and me.

We spent evenings shoulder-to-shoulder turning pages and gazing at all the toys. She would focus on the dolls, and I would zero in on the horse-related items.

I made a list and then changed my mind. *Did I want the miniature barn with farm animals, especially the horses, or a picture book of horses or the Barbie doll with a trunk with dresses?* I let Santa choose.

By the second week of December, it was time to decorate our Cape Cod's front windows.

Mom retrieved the stencils from the attic and spread the nativity scene, angels, Santa, his sleigh and reindeer, snowmen, and snowflakes on the kitchen table. Roni orchestrated the event.

"Kathy, don't touch anything. I want to draw the hills and inn on the living room window first, and then you can help me color them in," Roni commanded.

"Okay," I said a little downhearted.

While Roni was working on the front window, I ran back into the kitchen. I grabbed Santa, his sleigh, reindeer, and tape and proceeded to the dining room window. I was quite happy taping the stencils where I wanted them!

"What are you doing?" Roni called out. "Bring the tape."

"I'm coming," I called back.

With tape in hand, I ran into the living room and saw Roni holding the Nativity stencil on the window.

"Hurry up. I can't wait to color this," she said.

"I want to color too," I whined as I taped the stencil on four sides.

Once it was completed, we proceeded to the dining room.

"You got the sleigh crooked and Santa is too high," Roni complained. "Plus, I want to draw the snow scene first."

"Mom," I wailed. "Roni won't let me color."

"Let Kathy color," Mom said.

From then on, things went better, and we finished our "Picasso!"

This year, it was Roni's and my turn to stay at Nana and Grandpa's house for a few days. Mike and David would visit next year (having four grandchildren overnight would test anyone's sanity).

Christmas was not complete without a trip downtown and pictures with Santa.

First, our grandparents took us to the Sears department store to have pictures taken with Santa. It was crowded with shoppers eager to see the wonderful decorations that were similar to our malls today, but less grandiose.

The next day, we went downtown to view the shopkeepers' windows. They were decorated in holiday scenes and some had Nativities (back then they were not banned from public view). To top off the day, we had lunch and fudge sundaes at the malt shop.

It was always a magical time with our grandparents!

But my fondest family tradition was the hunt for the Christmas tree with Mom and Dad. We bundled up in our warmest clothes and coats and looked like stuffed cabbages with appendages of boots, hats, and mittens.

Dad held Mom's gloved hand as he led us out on our seven-acre wooded haven. Pines, cedars, oaks, and holly trees adorned with red berries greeted us.

It didn't take long for our cherub cheeks to turn crimson from the cold, frosty air.

"How about this one, kids?" Dad teased.

"No Dad; it looks like Charlie Brown's," I replied with a sigh.

As we pushed on deeper into the woods, laughter, sometimes silence, an occasional snap of a twig, and "crunch, crunch" was heard as we stepped on leaves mingled with clumps of icy snow. Gradually, as our fingers and toes began to ache, we became less and less selective.

"Dad, we like this one," we shouted. The pine dusted with snow looked just fine to us.

Looking back now, most of our Christmas trees were spindly, but it didn't matter because I was spending time with my dad.

On Christmas Eve, five stockings were hung on the mantel. They were made of red felt and our names were written on the white trim. The tree was prominently placed in its stand in the front window and then adorned with Christmas lights, balls, and icicles.

Back then, I liked to venture outside at night to view our home and the twinkling stars frozen in the dark abyss above it. There is a faint glow from the kitchen. Stenciled art work runs along the bottom of the windows. Through the multi-colored, lit tree, I see my dad asleep in his favorite chair hugging a pillow that is also perched under his chin. Firelight dances on the wall behind him. I know my mother with apron embracing her waist is cooking dinner. I am engulfed in darkness until I can no longer ignore the cold. I run into the house and wait for tomorrow's nightfall to beckon me once again.

Recalling this event brings immeasurably joy, peace, and a few tears. I miss my parents so much.

Recently, one evening, when I was at the sink cleaning apples and admiring their color and firmness, an inexpressible feeling of being immensely blessed covered me. It felt like ashes floating softly from an autumn leaf fire and then settling on my shoe or being warmed by a soft blanket after jumping into bed with cold sheets.

Without realizing it, as a child, I mixed the comfort of blessings—family, food, home, a warm fire—with the growing excitement of Christmas' arrival. I anticipated going to midnight mass and celebrating baby Jesus' birth as much as Santa's arrival.

I stood in the kitchen and welcomed another wave of memories as it washed over me.

Every Christmas Eve we dressed in our best outfits and, along the way to church, we saw houses adorned with lights and candles in the windows. Some of the homes had reindeer and Santa in his sleigh, snowmen or a Nativity outside. As we passed, we uttered oohs and ahhs.

Upon entering the parking lot, I saw the life-sized Nativity and the church's stained glass windows outlined from the amber glow of lights within. As we walked through the vestibule, we were welcomed by parishioners singing carols. I looked at pine sprays with red ribbons placed on window sills and the altar adorned in linen. Candles flickered, and the story of Christ's birth was read.

When we arrived home, we went to our bedrooms, changed into pajamas, jumped into bed and tried to go to sleep.

As dawn squinted through the blinds, Roni and I woke and then scampered downstairs to see what Santa brought us. We saw our stockings bulging with an orange, apple and candy canes. One gift from Santa greeted us.

Santa brought me a horse farm with barn, fences, five plastic horses and one miniature saddle and bridle. Roni received a Barbie doll dressed in a red velvet gown with a matching cape that was trimmed with white satin. We were both overjoyed.

Of course, we couldn't keep quiet for long. As Mike and David dashed down the stairs, they saw their gifts. David got a microscope and Mike got his first bike!

With all the whooping and hollering, my parents awakened. And then baby Mary Ellen cried. While Mom tended to Mary Ellen, Dad brewed the coffee. With coffee cups in hand, they settled on the sofa to open presents.

Each of us usually had two wrapped gifts under the tree. To stretch out the event, presents were opened one at a time for all to admire before the next child opened his or her gifts. We had clothes from Nana, Grandpa, and Grandma. Aunt Mildred provided the Russell Stover's chocolates.

After presents were opened, Mom and Dad prepared dinner. The aroma of stuffed turkey cooking penetrated the house and made our tummies rumble. Finally, it was time to eat. The turkey was on the middle of the table with dishes of peas, crescent rolls, and mashed potatoes surrounding it. The pumpkin pies were on the countertop behind our Christmas meal. All heads bowed and the blessing was recited. Our feast was heavenly.

As darkness descended on our festivities, I slipped outside to perform my nightly vigil and thanked God for blessings as only a five-year-old could.

By today's standards, our 1960's Christmas might appear meager, but I knew I was loved, and that is the best gift of all.

Thank You, God, for providing Christian parents who introduced me to my Lord, Jesus, at an early age. I am grateful for my parents and for all of their sacrifices so Mike, David, Roni, Mary Ellen, Julie and I had every thing we needed and more.

The Gift of Christmas

Barbara Creath Foster

For God so loved the world,
that He gave His only begotten Son,
that whosoever believeth in Him should not perish,
but have everlasting life.
John 3:16 KJV

All our lives, we have been told it is more blessed to give than ro receive. But before Christmas some of us spend time anticipating what we will get on the big day. Especially children, who look forward to lots of presents. Little boys dream of trucks and drums. And the girls want dolls and all the things Santa might bring.

When I was growing up, my brother, sister, and I received toys and games and books and things like that for Christmas. We did not get anything as expensive as my friends did or as many presents as some of our cousins. But we did get fabulous presents from New York

City. One aunt and uncle lived in New Jersey near the big city stores in NYC. I always looked forward to the gifts Aunt Gertrude would send because she sent us unusual things—great toys Santa didn't bring. We spent many days playing with the toys and games she sent. Later, when we became teenagers, she sent sweaters and hats and things we proudly wore. None of my friends had presents from New York City. Such merchandize didn't exist in our small town.

I figured Aunt Gertrude spent more money on us than Santa Claus. What I didn't know was that my family wasn't rich. It wasn't until I grew up that I realized our family income back then was below the poverty level. I knew my father didn't make as much money as some other fathers. But that didn't matter. The word "poor" was never mentioned. We never lacked essential things like food, clothing, and shelter. And love. We never lacked love. Our home was filled with love. Lots of Love. We were as good as anybody and everybody else.

When I told a good friend about my childhood situation, she said, "That was a great gift your parents gave you, one of the greatest gifts they could have given you." As I thought about what she said, I realized that the gift has stayed with me all these years. I still don't have much money. But I'm not poor. I'm rich surrounded with love.

We get gifts that glitter and glow
In fancy paper with a bow.
God gave us the greatest present
Wrapped in a joyous event.
It happened the first Christmas morn
When God's son, Jesus Christ, was born.

Jesus is the best gift—the greatest one God can give us. Because Christ died on the cross to deliver us from our sins, and if we believe and repent, we will have the eternal life promised in the Bible. What can be greater than God's perfect present?

The best gifts aren't the things we buy and wrap up in fancy paper. They are the things we give from our hearts and the things we do for others, all wrapped up in our love. So maybe, instead of shopping in crowded stores for the elusive perfect present, we should be thinking of ways to give of ourselves this Christmas.

It was on the bright morn of Jesus' birth
That God gave us love, joy, and peace on earth.
Let's remember—Jesus is the reason
We celebrate this holiday season.

Mystery Gift

Judi Folmsbee

*But the Spirit produces the fruit of love, joy, peace, patience, kindness,
goodness, faithfulness, gentleness, and self-control.
There is no law that says these things are wrong.*
Galatians 5:22-23 NCV

While standing in the doorway of my first-grade classroom, I saw Jeff skipping down the hall, waving his hands, smiling, and shouting in a song-like voice.

"Look! Look! I have your Christmas present!" He flung his hand with the package in it in my direction and pranced around like a proud pony.

As I received the gift, I turned the package, gently shaking it so as not to break anything. I remember saying, "I wonder what this could be? Boy, Jeff, you worked hard wrapping this." Before I ripped off the first piece of paper and wad of tape, Jeff said proudly, "It took me all night."

I was in a dilemma, I did not want to laugh at him or hurt his feelings, but what kind of gift was this? It was a rectangular box, twelve inches wide, wrapped with crumpled Pokémon paper and held together with mountains of tape. Fastened to the wrapping paper was the white plastic torso of an action figure with black and red marker ink all over it. The torso was accompanied by a small brown plastic ladder. In addition, pieces of plastic straws in various lengths and colors were strategically placed.

When I opened the package, I was speechless. Inside was an empty Mueller's Italian style jumbo shells box. The top of the box was taped closed. It took me a few minutes to realize that this empty box with all the various ornaments on the outside was his gift. *How could this be a serious gift?* It occurred to me that this was a real gift of the heart. This is what he could give.

Jeff was not afraid to share. Where was the gift in this box? Was it hiding from me? Yes! He was sharing the best of his gifts. It was more sincere than some gifts I have received, or some given, for that matter. I had to take a deep, long look into the empty box to realize that. It was filled to the brim with love, kindness, caring, vulnerability, trust, and sharing.

Jeff did not have any fancy package or state-of-the-art gift. This gift was overflowing with more than money could buy.

Lord, thank You for putting children in our lives to remind us what the important things are as we travel this road of life. Help us to recognize the true value of gifts from the heart.

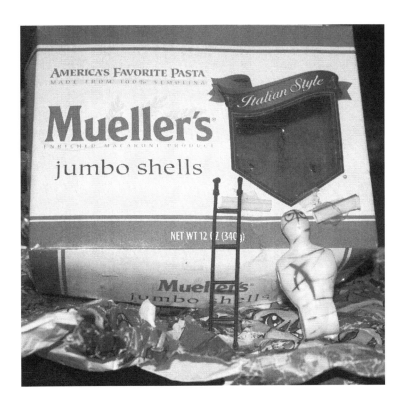

A Royal Celebration

Lori Ciccanti

"Where is the one who has been born king of the Jews?
We saw his star in the east and have come to worship him."
On coming to the house,
[the Magi] saw the child with his mother Mary,
and they bowed down and worshipped him.
Then they opened their treasures and presented him with gifts
of gold and of incense and of myrrh.
Matthew 2:2, 11 NIV

On January sixth, many people in the Spanish culture celebrate what is known as *El Dia De Los Tres Reyes Majos* or *Three Kings Day*. As a child, I was amazed to hear my mother tell stories of how she observed this special holiday. Surprisingly, in her family tradition, this occasion was even more eventful than Christmas. Later, I realized how the custom of gift-giving on Three Kings Day may actually be more suitable in drawing attention to the birth of Jesus rather than the hustle and bustle of a busy, more commercialized Christmas season.

Yet, contrary to tradition, the Bible record does not say that the Magi were kings or how many followed the star. Interestingly, their background connects them to the prophet Daniel who was "chief of the magicians" in Babylon. These Magi, although considered wise, were not able to interpret King Nebuchadnezzar's dream *(see Daniel 2:5,24)*, even at the risk of losing their lives. Therefore, Daniel saved them from the king's murderous wrath when he demonstrated the Lord's power by revealing both the dream and its prophetic meaning. As a result, future generations of Magi became familiar with the Hebrew prophecies, and when the star appeared to them, they understood that it meant the birth of an extraordinary king.

Although the giving of gifts was in keeping with oriental tradition, most would agree that the gifts presented to Jesus had a deeper, more profound significance. How fitting that gold, most precious of all metals, be given to the One who was born King. Frankincense, an expensive aromatic resin, was said to have medicinal properties and was even used to treat depression in the ancient world. It was also burned for its calming aroma in temple worship and other special occasions; hence, it represents the priestly ministry of Christ. Myrrh, the most unusual of the three gifts, is derived from a tough tree that grows in the semi-desert climate of North Africa. It was used as an antiseptic and embalming ointment that reminds us of our Lord's great sacrifice.

After pondering the wonderful meaning of our Savior's gifts, I was struck by a beautiful Christmas card I received from a friend. It read something like this:

*You are cordially invited
to join in the Royal Celebration
of the Savior of the World.*

WHAT:
THE BIRTH OF OUR SAVIOR JESUS CHRIST
(ISAIAH 9:6; LUKE 2:11)

WHO:
ALL ARE INVITED TO CELEBRATE
(MATTHEW 11:28; JOHN 14:6)

WHEN:
THE CELEBRATION IS EVERY DAY
(PSALM 145:2)

WHERE:
THE CELEBRATION BEGINS IN YOUR HEART
(ROMANS 10:9-10; JOHN 3:16)

THIS INVITATION IS EXTENDED TO ALL PEOPLE EVERYWHERE WHO ARE WILLING TO FOLLOW THE EXAMPLE OF THE MAGI. HOPEFULLY, YOU WILL NOT MISS THIS GREAT OPPORTUNITY TO CELEBRATE THE ONE WHO WAS BORN KING OF KINGS; COME WITH THE MOST PRECIOUS GIFT OF ALL—YOUR HEART.

PLEASE R.S.V.P.

O Lord our King, we humbly acknowledge the royal invitation that is ours to seek Your awesome presence and worship before Your throne of grace. Like the wise men, may we give no less than our very best, loving You always with all our soul, strength, and mind. In Jesus' holy name, we pray.

Remembering

Mary Emma Tisinger

❧

I remember the day you left.
I remember the wind,
so wild,
and that icy cold feeling
not only outdoors,
my heart was chilled as well.

I remember the long walk
through the corridor,
while *Silent Night* filled the air
and Christmas trees twinkled
all around;
reminding me
that Christmas will never be
the same.

Karen H. Whiting

Figure out the words for the search from these clues. Circle the words within the puzzle based on the clues. Place the uncircled letters on the dotted lines to find a message.

```
E   M   R   E   G   N   A   M   B   E
L   O   R   A   C   S   U   S   E   J
C   R   R   P   R   O   H   E   T   S
R   Y   C   C   H   E   R   R   H   I
I   R   A   T   S   T   D   S   L   N
C   A   N   D   Y   C   A   N   E   O
A   A   D   V   E   N   T   E   H   E
R   T   L   G   A   B   R   I   E   L
D   M   E   A   N   G   E   L   M   A
```

1. Candy made in shape of a shepherd's staff
2. Christmas color for love.
3. Christmas color for everlasting.
4. Men who told about the coming of Jesus.
5. Angel who spoke to Mary.
6. Town where Jesus was born.
7. The word means "coming." (Time before Christmas).
8. We light these in a wreath.
9. The shape of a wreath.

10. Christmas is his birthday.
11. The wise men followed this.
12. Greeting mailed to people.
13. Who told shepherds about Jesus.
14. Songs sung at Christmas.
15. Jesus was laid in this.
16. French word for Christmas (The First __ __ __ __)

__ __ __ __ __ __ __ __ __ __ __ __ __ S

ANSWER KEY

(No peeking, please, until you're finished with the puzzle)

MERRY CHRISTMAS

1. CANDY CANE
2. RED
3. GREEN
4. PROPHETS
5. GABRIEL
6. BETHLEHEM
7. ADVENT
8. CANDLE
9. CIRCLE
10. JESUS
11. STAR
12. CARD
13. ANGEL
14. CAROL
15. MANGER
16. NOEL

Fullness

Gail Atlas

For God was pleased to have all his fullness dwell in him,
and through him to reconcile to himself all things,
whether things on earth or things in heaven,
by making peace through his blood, shed on the cross.

Colossians 1:19-20 NIV

It was beyond distressing. I came home from Sunday school that morning in early December 1972, wanting to cry or scream or maybe even throw something. I loved teaching the five year olds, but this Sunday, all they wanted to talk about was Santa Claus, Santa Claus, Santa Claus! My adult leader didn't seem bothered by it, which added to my frustration. I was seventeen. Four months earlier, after attending church since babyhood, I had finally realized who Jesus is: the Son of God, the Messiah, my Savior. In His quiet but powerful way, God had called me into His kingdom, forcing me to admit my sinful nature, my failure to honor Him with the life He had given me. And now, as I contemplated my first celebration of His Incarnation with His intimate indwelling, the kids were completely focused on a legend they thought was real. I vowed right then that if I ever had children, they would never believe in Santa Claus.

Years later, after I married, my husband readily agreed to this. Having grown up nominally Jewish, he had no personal connection to the mythical character. We set out to make Christmas about the wonder of God becoming man. What a magnificent reason to celebrate. Of course, we gave presents, since Christmas recalls God's free gift of reconciliation through His Son. And I like the idea of giving my children a gift because I love them, rather than a stranger giving them something because they are "naughty or nice."

Of course, there are some funny, slightly embarrassing stories because of our decision. One time as we checked our packages out in a department store, the well-meaning cashier asked our four-year-old daughter what she wanted Santa to bring her that year. Our daughter, precocious anyway, but seemingly more so because she looked at least a year younger than she actually was, shocked the poor lady. "Santa Claus is dead," she said with a patronizing look. "He lived many years ago and gave gifts to poor people," referring to the story of Saint Nicholas.

Many people have managed to fit Santa into their celebrations and still emphasize Jesus. For me, this way has worked better. There was no loss of amazement when the kids "found out," because the awe of Christmas has always been in the Truth. In fact, as I grow older, that astonishment continues to grow as I see more of the greatness of God and the depravity of this world—how could He leave what He had for this? I only pray that those now-grown children from my Sunday school class—and all I have connected with over the years— have come to embrace this true wonder of Christmas, accepting no substitutes for God, in all His fullness, becoming man.

Silent Angel

Betty Lewis Kasperski

"Mommy, Mommy, when are we going to put up our tree? Christmas is in just two days," Missy asked.

"Tomorrow afternoon, when I get home from work." I assured her. "You and David have everything ready from the closet, and we will do it then."

"Great, Mommy. I can't wait for Christmas."

As I viewed her bright brown eyes brimming with enthusiasm, my heart ached. Yes, we had the tree and decorations, but I had nothing to put under the tree for my loving children, eight-year-old Missy, and six-year-old David.

Three years ago, Roy, my husband and the children's father, decided that marriage and "daddy hood" was not for him; he disappeared to find his true soul in the mountains of Colorado. A few "me-centered" phone calls came the first six weeks and then nothing. Support was a sparse four hundred dollars a month and then that also terminated. Besides being devastated that he could just walk away from all of us, I instantly became a single parent and sole breadwinner, a role that I had not expected to play. I moved forward and got a second job, but last month a pre-winter cold snap hit the east coast and the utility bill skyrocketed. I was barely keeping up before that. Then, an unexpected car repair of over four hundred dollars evaporated any cushion of funds I had managed to squirrel away.

I tried to remain positive and not filled with anger, but disappointing my kids made me boil inside. It wasn't fair. We are good people. Families should be families and not just wander off.

"Janet," I told myself, "We can only control our own behavior, not that of others and many folks will disappoint you." But abandoning these precious babies was unacceptable, unforgivable. I prayed for a calm spirit, for a Christmas angel to appear, not for me, but for Missy and David. They deserved a real Christmas.

"What time will you be home, Mommy?" David asked.

"When the big hand is on the twelve and the little hand is on the three." I responded, pointing to the clock above the kitchen sink.

"Hurry home, Mommy. Auntie Claire said that we can make some extra decorations with her while you are at work. I am going to make an angel for the top of the tree."

"Great, David. We don't have anything for the top of the tree."

"What are you going to make, Missy?"

"I want to make a garland from popcorn. Just like the one in the picture book."

"A wonderful idea. We have two bags of popcorn, you can eat one and decorate with the other."

"Go, Mommy, so you can come back soon." David echoed.

"After we do the tree, we can ride around and see all the houses decorated with bright holiday lights before we go to church for the Christmas Eve service. See you later. Love you Missy. Love you David."

"Love you, Mom." They chimed.

Their enthusiasm was so infectious; I, too, believed Christmas was coming for us. Still, I didn't know how that would happen. But a miracle was coming our way. When we returned from the Christmas Eve service, not only did our tree glisten on the far side of the room, but also underneath the tree, a dozen presents had arrived. Little items for all of us. Name tags said who they were for but not who they were from.

I questioned Aunt Claire but she said, "No, it must have been a Christmas angel who knew that Missy, David, and you had been very, very good and had made the list."

I tried to find out who had deposited those gifts of love for us, but no one knew. About four years later, Aunt Claire confessed to her good deed but said that she had been prompted "to just do it and be silent." She felr our special family should get some little love gifts, reflecting God's love—the biggest Christmas gift of all.

Every year, from the time when my children were only eight and six years old until now when they are thirty eight and thirty six, I have adopted a family and silently supplied their Christmas. I never knew where those extra dollars were coming from, but somehow those funds arrived just in time for me to share and surprise another family with a quiet representation of God's love, as their silent Christmas angel.

The Shepherd

Gail Atlas

Was it the same man? No, he looked too young. But he had the same power about him—the power this former shepherd had felt, even in that tiny Infant so many years ago. He drew closer to the man talking. The crowds were thick, each straining to hear the wisdom he shared. Some were taking in his message, their faces knotted, thinking. Some were laughing, and some were ridiculing. Still others were arguing and bantering back and forth with the man.

The shepherd had been in Athens long enough to know the ways of the people there. They loved to listen to new ideas. They would dispute everything from the shape and size of the world to what happens to animals when they die. It all seemed silly to the shepherd. He had questions, too, but his questions were different. His all went back to one night, the night that changed his life.

It started off as an ordinary night. He had just turned ten, an important milestone in his community. When a boy turned ten, he was old enough to go with the men at night. That meant no more staying around the village and being tormented. You see, his people, the shepherds, weren't liked much among the villagers. Oh, they wanted the sheep and lambs for the Passover, but they didn't want anything to do with the people who kept them. Many times he had been called "dirty shepherd" before he even touched a sheep. But now he was going regularly with the older men to watch the sheep all night. Their job was important, even if they were not esteemed. They had to make sure the sheep were kept from harm, kept pure, to be used for the annual slaughtering.

So that night, that special night, the shepherd had packed his small bag with cheese and bread. He had taken his staff and his rod, each cut to his size. He was getting good at using the curved staff to bring a wandering lamb back. The rod he hadn't used yet, but he was sure he could club a lion if it threatened one of his sheep. He walked silently with the other men to the field, thinking of all the potential dangers he might face, thinking what a hero he could be. He would be like David, the shepherd of old who became a king. Well, he could never become a king, because the Romans didn't let the Jews be kings anymore. But he could be brave like David, and his people would hail him as a hero, a great shepherd who saved the flock . . .

The young shepherd jolted awake, still on his feet. They had reached the field and were finding their places. All daydreams aside, he admitted the hardest thing about being a shepherd was staying awake. It was dark, and there had been other chores do to during the day. The sheep grazed in the grass, not needing much attention. The other shepherds had their routines. Some talked quietly about adult things. Some played harps or flutes, but he had heard their songs before. He gazed at the stars overhead. Sometimes even they seemed to be telling a story he could almost make out. Tonight all was quiet, and he pinched himself to stay awake.

What, what was that? It was so bright. He instinctively put up his hand to shield his eyes from the brightness. But it was more than brilliance. His whole body shook. His eyes peeped out from between his fingers, afraid of what he might see. Then, he heard a voice, the voice. The one he would never forget. "Do not be afraid." *How did the voice know?* "I bring you good news of great joy that will be for all the people" (Luke 2:10). The voice went on to describe a Baby, and then there were many voices, filling the sky and the earth, glorifying God. As the young shepherd took his hand from his eyes, wonder overrode the fear and intensity. He was vaguely aware of the other shepherds, their mouths open and their eyes wide. No one seemed to breathe or move, absorbing every sight and sound: great light, wings fluttering, music fuller than any instrument, "Glory, glory, glory to God!"

And then it was silent. Still. Dark. Yet, not as dark as it had been. The shepherds began to talk, quietly at first, then more insistent.

"Let's go," they decided.

And leaving the sheep, they went, the young shepherd leading the way with all the energy of his youth. They found the cave and once again they were quiet. They tiptoed in and found the Baby and His parents, all the way the angel had said. The oldest shepherd began, and then the rest of them couldn't help but share what they had witnessed: how the angels came, how one had described this very scene. The young parents smiled but didn't seem surprised.

The young shepherd stared at the Child. Something about Him made the ten-year-old feel tiny and yet enlarged at the same time. This Baby was God, the Messiah, the angel had said. The shepherd knew it was true. He felt dirty. The memory of all the wrongs he had ever done weighed him down. But as he looked at the Baby—and he couldn't turn his eyes away—he knew it didn't matter anymore. Somehow, this Infant made it all right. It was as if a barrier had been lifted. Words of David poured from his heart: "Blessed is the one whose transgressions are forgiven, whose sins are covered. Blessed is the one whose sin the Lord does not count against them" (Psalm 31:1-2).

The joy of it all compelled him out of the small cave. He had to tell others. Everyone he met heard his story, not just that night, but from then on. People thought him crazy, crazier still as he kept at it. That's what brought him to Athens. Because he really wasn't a shepherd anymore. His own people had tired of hearing about that night. He had gone from town to town, great distances from his people. No one cared about his story.

But now, here in the Aeropagus, listening to this scholar, he knew. This man would understand. He waited for the crowds to thin and approached the short man. Small in stature, yes, but what a powerful message. Yet, just like no one wanted to listen to the ex-shepherd, most were turning away from this man, not at all heeding what he said.

"Sir," began the former shepherd. "You said, 'God did this so that [people] would seek Him and perhaps reach out for Him and find Him, though He is not far from any one of us' (Acts 17:27). I know this is true." He told the story of that night. "Can you tell me what happened to that Child?" he finished.

"Where have you been since then?" the man asked him.

"Everywhere. I've been as far as Spain. But no one would listen."

"Perhaps you should have stayed home," the preacher smiled. "But I will tell you what you missed." He proceeded to tell about Jesus' life and death, ending with the same words with which he concluded his prior speech: "[God] has set a day when He will judge the world with justice by the Man he has appointed. He has given proof of this to everyone by raising Him from the dead" (Acts 17:31).

"Raised from the dead? So He still lives? I knew it. I knew it! That Child could not die!"

With further understanding, a new man emerged from that encounter. A new man, with a story that people did listen to. Once again, he was a shepherd. But this time, he gathered people to guide and protect rather than sheep.

Family Activities to Focus on Jesus this Christmas

Karen H. Whiting

Christmas is about Jesus coming. He loves us so much that He chose to become a baby, grow up, and die, so we can go to heaven. Christmas is such a busy time with parties and gifts that we forget Jesus. We can seem like the innkeeper who had no room for Him. Take time to remember Jesus. Try a few of these activities:

- Light the advent wreath each day and sing a Christmas carol (one about Jesus like *Silent Night* or *Away in a Manger*).

- Buy clothes and baby toys you would really want Jesus to wear and play with and give them to a shelter.

- Read about the birth of Jesus in the Bible and then act it out.

- Look at the stars one night. Think about how the one the wise men followed must have looked.

- Take one figure of the nativity set each day and talk about how that fits in with the birth of Jesus and the importance of it.

- Wrap Christmas videos and books and place them under the tree by December 1. Every few days open one and enjoy it as a family.

- Decorate your door (or bedroom door) to welcome Jesus.

- Do kind acts for Jesus each day by helping other people.

- Have a Christmas caroling night of singing Christmas songs that are about Jesus.

- Write a letter to Jesus thanking him for coming.

- Say, "Have a Blessed Christmas," or "Jesus is the reason for the season" to people.

- Pass out candy canes (little shepherd staffs) and remind people that Jesus came to be our shepherd.

- Decorate a birthday cake (or cupcake) for Jesus and sing happy birthday.

- Play flashlight hide and seek. Turn off the lights and let everyone hide except the seeker. That person uses a flashlight to find the others.

A Christmas Wonder

Michele Jones

I wonder what it was like on that most holy night
The world unaware
As quietly He lay
In a cold, stone manger filled with hay
The stars shone brightly above
While here upon the earth
The Incarnate Son
The fullness of God's love
Sent to bring restoration
Reuniting God and man
Through Christ

I wonder what it was like on that most glorious night
With angels proclamations
Resounding throughout the skies
Good news and great joy for all generations
This is the Christ Child
Who has been sent to save us

I wonder did she hear the angels sing
as she cradled this new born King?
Holding tiny hands that formed the universe
Kissing tiny feet that would break the curse
The serpent's head He would crush
In order that He might save us
Did His sleepy eyes reflect the stars that blanketed the heavens above?
Stars He himself had placed; He had named each one

I wonder would all of the prophecies about Him
Begin to flood her mind
As she rocked her newborn baby
on that most holy night
He had been spoken of and foreshadowed
since the beginning of time
Things that once had been pondered
were they coming to life?

The Godhead
Three-In-One
Now fast asleep He lay cradled in her arms
How could the fullness of deity
Leave heaven's realm to offer us peace?
How could this tiny Child know it was Him we seek?
How could the radiance of God's glory
Take on flesh and become human?

Because God had a plan
We were the reason
Jesus
A Royal Priest
Our awaited King
He is the Chosen One
To us salvation He would bring

One whose name we would joyfully worship
And our ransomed souls do forever sing
Holy
Holy
Holy
Is the Lord God Almighty
Who was and is and is to come
Our Sovereign King
Most Righteous One

This seemingly helpless Child
Would soon turn the world upside down
For by His birth we have found new worth
He set a plan in motion
That would thwart the enemy's schemes and notions
He would break the chains of bondage
And set the captives free
For it was His life He would sacrifice
To give us the GIFT of eternal life
He died for us upon that cross
To bridge the gap with hope
And restore all those who are lost

The world unaware
while quietly He waits
just beyond the heavenly gates
for man to turn and seek His face
The mystery is revealed
And by His blood we are sealed
To commune with Him
And self-forsake
To love our brother and our neighbor
To boldly walk in faith
For the day is soon coming
For His triumphant returning
I wonder . . . do you remember a Baby?
Or, do you wait for a King?

From the Manger to the Cross

David Michael Smith

Every Sunday morning many Christians of Catholic and Anglican faith, as well as most Protestant denominations throughout the earth, faithfully recite the Nicene Creed during worship of the Holy Triune God above all other gods.

That recitation, boldly spoken in a singular unified voice, and while standing as one body, and facing the altar and cross, is a public affirmation and pronouncement of our beliefs as the Church. It represents the key elements of our commonality within the various denominations and church houses regarding what we believe in our hearts as Christians. These are "truth statements" that are not debatable, and cannot be argued away by modern day theories and watered down hypocrisies.

Part of the Creed states:

For us men and for our salvation,
He came down from heaven:
He was incarnate by the Holy Spirit of the Virgin Mary,
And was made man.
For our sake he was crucified under Pontius Pilate;
He suffered death and was buried.

On the third day He rose again in fulfillment of the Scriptures;
He ascended into heaven,
And is seated at the right hand of the Father.
He will come again in glory to judge the living and the dead,
And His kingdom will have no end.

Every story has a beginning and an ending. The Nicene Creed captures the start of the Messiah's time on earth as incarnate man, at Christmas, born as an innocent, sweet baby in a lowly barn, not a stately palace, mind you, which would've been fit for the King that He was and is today. And the end of the story is Easter, the Holy Passion of Jesus Christ that included his arrest, persecution, crucifixion and finally, His incredible, beautiful resurrection on the third day!

But the Christian story, our story, has no real ending. Our God will reign forever and ever, and as His followers, baptized and redeemed and adopted, we will inherit that same blessed everlasting life! That being said, let us more closely examine the beginning of this story, Christmas, which we now celebrate every December 25, and the ending, Easter, the painful, agonizing death and rebirth of our Lord. Each part of the story is connected and supports the other.

Easter needs Christmas and Christmas needs Easter. Without the Easter miracle, Jesus becomes just another boy born into poverty, a great and kind teacher and a good man, but Lord of lords? And without Christmas, without the incarnate arrival of the Son of God, you cannot have Easter. Otherwise, who was that man on the cross and why would He be important to the history of mankind? Each season, each special event, needs the other. Christmas and Easter are eternally connected.

There are many wonderful, melodic Christmas carols which we sing during the holiday season. Everyone has his or her own favorites, tunes like *Silent Night, O Come All Ye Faithful, Away in the Manger,* and secular ones such as *Jingle Bells* and *The Christmas Song.* But at Easter the list is shorter. There is, however, one very powerful song, an old, simple spiritual, which is typically sung on Good Friday of Holy Week, *Were You There* (When They Crucified My Lord).

What if these two connected events in history could be forever yoked together musically in the framework of this Eastertide song? Christmas, the advent of the story of God Almighty embodied, and Easter, the final act, but really, the new beginning, and our reason for the season of Christmas. Rejoice!

Were you there on the night our Lord was born?
Were you there on the night that Christ was born?
Oh . . . O Come, O Come Emmanuel,
Rejoice, rejoice, Emmanuel, shall come to these O Israel.

Were you there with the shepherds and the sheep?
Were you there when baby Jesus fell asleep?
Oh . . . O Little Town of Bethlehem, how still we see thee lie,
Above thy deep and dreamless sleep, the silent stars go by.

Were you there when the wise men came to see?
Were you there when they came on bended knee?
Oh . . . O Star of wonder, star of night,
Star with royal beauty bright,
Westward leading, still proceeding,
Guide us to thy perfect light.

And were you there on the hillside when he preached?
Were you there on the mountain when he teached?
    Oh . . . no, no . . . Noel, Noel, Noel, Noel,
    Born is the King of Israel.

Were you there when He broke the loaf and said,
"Remember Me when you eat this holy bread,"
Oh . . . O holy night, the stars are brightly shining,
    This is the night of our dear Savior's birth.

And were you there when they crucified my Lord?
Were you there when they crucified our Lord?
    Oh . . . O come let us adore Him,
        O come let us adore Him,
    O Come let us adore Him, Christ the Lord!

And were you there when he rose up from the tomb?
Were you there when he forever defeated doom?
    Oh . . . glo . . . Gloria, in excelsis deo,
        Gloria, in excelsis deo!
    Angels we have heard on high,
    Sweetly singing over the plains,
    And the mountains in reply,
    Echoing their joyous strains,
    Gloria . . . in excelsis deo,
    Gloria . . . in excelsis deo!

And will you be there when we gather at His throne?
Will you be there when we gather at His throne?

And the saints will sing:

> *King of kings, forever and ever,*
> *And Lord of lords, forever and ever,*
> *Hallelujah! Hallelujah! Hallelujah! Hallelujah!*

In the book of Luke, chapter 2, it's written, beginning at the tenth verse, "Then the angel said to the shepherds, "Do not be afraid, for behold, I bring you good tidings of great joy which will be to all people. For there is born to you this day in the city of David a Savior, who is Christ the Lord!'"

And He, the Son of God; He, the Prince of Peace; He, the Lord of lords and King of kings; He, the promised and prophesied Messiah; He, the Great I Am, the Alpha and the Omega, the Anointed one of Israel, the perfect sacrifice, the Lamb of God, the Wonderful Counselor and God of mercy and love . . . and He . . . the little innocent infant in a simple wooden manger, yes, He shall reign forevermore!

To sum it up, a famous theologian, Linus Van Pelt, once was asked about the true meaning of Christmas and he quoted the same passage from Luke. Then as he exited the stage, he quietly said to his friend, "That's what Christmas is all about, Charlie Brown."

A New Dawn

Candy Abbott

We felt more like Santa's elves than choir members. The table was strewn with gifts we had bought to surprise a family we'd never met. Our chatter competed with the crinkle of Christmas paper and the fragrance of gingerbread and fresh coffee.

"This is for the mother. Her name is Dawn, right?" Jane asked. "And her husband's in prison? Here's a gift for him."

"This one's for Chandra," I said. "She's two. And the baby girl's name is Felicia."

Margaret chimed in. "By the way, who's going to deliver the gifts? Would you do it, Candy?"

"Sure," I said weakly, wondering how I would feel if I were a struggling mother who may or may not be receptive to charity. As soon as I agreed, the choir loaded four leaf bags of wrapped gifts into my car along with a basket of canned goods and a frozen turkey. It's one thing to buy and wrap presents anonymously. It's another to deliver them face-to-face.

Dawn didn't have a phone, so I couldn't call in advance. I drove to her trailer unannounced, with sweaty palms and my stomach turning flip flops. *Get a grip,* I told myself. *This is a needy family, and you're delivering bags full of joy.*

I pulled into muddy ruts which served as a driveway and parked behind a rusty vehicle. The cold night air chilled me to the bone as I turned off the engine and opened the car door. With trembling fingers, I reached into the back seat for one of the bags. My timid knock on the rickety door was answered by a slender woman with long brown hair, wide eyes with a stunned look and a pale but pretty face. Some sort of explanation tumbled out of me as I inched the cumbersome bags onto the doorstep. Dawn was hesitant but accepted the gifts with a nod of her head.

In her heartfelt thank-you note, she expressed an interest in attending worship services. Transportation was a problem, so Barbara offered to pick up Dawn and the girls on her way to church.

"But there's another problem," Barbara said. "She doesn't have anything to wear."

"You mean she needs something for church?"

Barbara paused. "I mean, she doesn't have *anything* to wear. She lives in her husband's holey t-shirts and flip flops, and I don't think she owns a winter coat. She doesn't even know what size she wears."

"Hmm," I smiled. "I think she's about my size. I have an attic full of clothes that just might do the trick."

Again, approaching Dawn's dirt road unannounced with a packed car, apprehension twisted my gut. *Clothing is much more personal than Christmas gifts. Please, Lord, don't let her be offended—and let them fit.*

Dawn's eyes were wide with wonder as she began pulling garments from the bag. On her, my old things looked brand new. That was the start of our "private recycling plan" and a 30-year friendship. I never comprehended how much my small kindnesses meant until years later when she said, "Candy, I didn't have a prayer. You don't know what it's like to feel trapped and not even know if there's a God out there to pray to. But God was there all along, and He used you and the church to answer prayers I didn't even know how to pray." She brushed away tears that rolled down her cheek.

"When you brought those first gifts from the choir, I'd been with my husband six or seven years. He controlled every aspect of my life—I had no birth control, no job, no friends. Things that people take for granted like clothes, shoes, and make-up weren't available to me. Then, after his release from prison, came the divorce. It was so hard for me to let go of something that was killing the children and me. But you came. You listened and allowed me the freedom to choose without judgment. Your gifts to me were self-esteem, confidence, and the sisterhood I so desperately needed. Best of all, you taught me how to pray."

Every year, our church made sure Dawn and her children had clothes for school and presents under the Christmas tree. One year, I tossed in an unwrapped book by Evelyn Christenson, *What Happens When Women Pray.*

"When I read that book," she said, "it was as though every light in the house came on. For the first time, I had hope. I couldn't do much, but I could *pray.*" She was too choked up to speak for a moment, and then explained. "That was the turning point for me. Somewhere in the middle of those pages, I committed my life to Christ. And then you invited me to a Sisters in Christ meeting in your home. It was there, in that safe, small-group setting that I learned to pray for others and found I could praise God with my whole heart."

Our Sisters in Christ had prayed for Dawn for a long time, so we rejoiced the first night she showed up. But she was painfully shy. When asked a question, she would act as if she hadn't heard or mumble an answer no one could understand. Making eye contact was absolute agony for her. Usually, she dashed out before the end of the meeting with her shoulders slumped and eyes downcast. But she came back, again and again. Then one evening in our prayer circle, Dawn's tender voice rang out with power and depth like none I had ever heard. It was as though her words had been bottled up and could stay corked no longer. When she whispered, "O holy God," it was as though the ceiling opened, and we were surrounded by angels.

Dawn has seen many answered prayers: From the courage it took for her to enroll in GED classes, to the day she and her children sought refuge in a shelter. From the joy of walking across the stage to receive her Associate Degree to the office job she held for over six years. And many unanswered prayers: From the agony of losing her teenage son in an auto accident, to sinking into years of depression and deteriorating health. Through it all, Dawn clung to her faith.

More than once she said, "Please, never give up on me." Every time, I assured her, "God never gives up on His children, and neither do I."

At fifty-five, Dawn's life came to an abrupt end on May 31, 2012. Unable to sleep, she walked from her apartment across the dual highway to a convenience store around four o'clock that foggy morning and was struck by a tractor trailer in the southbound lane. Her daughters asked me to sing *Amazing Grace,* at her memorial service. Every line resonated deeply as though it was not I, but Dawn singing them: "Thru many dangers, toils and snares I have already come; 'Tis grace hath brought me safe thus far, And grace *hath led* me home."

This story is not just about Dawn. It's about the lives she touched and the legacy she leaves in spite of a lifetime of difficult circumstances. Above all, she was a devoted mother and grandmother who openly shared her faith, as evidenced by her grandchildren reciting The Lord's Prayer at the close of her memorial service.

There is A New Dawn now, one who can view life from her heavenly perspective and say, "When I was hungry you fed me; when I was naked you clothed me." A New Dawn who can proclaim with eternal assurance that God's love never fails. He never gives up on "the least of these."

And to think—it all started with a family we had never met until that blessed Christmas that brought me bearing gifts from the choir to Dawn's humble doorstep.

What's that I hear? A heavenly choir of saints singing along with Dawn,

> *Holy, holy, holy*
> *is the Lord God Almighty,*
> *who was, and is, and is to come.*

God's Baby Boy

Cat Martin

Light is shining all around us.

The love that Christmas brings

lights up the lives of everyone.

A host of angels sing.

We cannot always understand

their songs of highest praise

as we try to make the best

of all our nights and days.

The Spirit shines brightly

to give us real peace and joy,

illuminating the face of Christ,

God's precious baby Boy.

One Christmas

Cat Martin

O ne Christmas, I was in a time of reflection. I thought about the experiences I'd had during that year, and the joys and sadness I knew others had experienced throughout their lives. Visions of violence and images of tear-stained faces came to my mind. I wondered how long human beings would continue being so cruel to one another. I was afraid. I wasn't in the best frame of mind to celebrate the season.

Then I thought of the angels, and I remembered their message and how they praised. I read the story of our Savior's birth in the Word. According to Luke, a host of angels praised God when Christ was born. God has given me the gift of seeing angels in dreams and visions. Each time I have seen an angel, I've experienced incredible peace and joy. I believe God would have each of us praise with as much enthusiasm as the angels praise.

Sometimes it's difficult because situations, events, and circumstances cloud my mind and attempt to prevent me from celebrating and experiencing the true meaning of Christmas. When this happens, I try to remember the angels and their promise to each of us. The victory comes when I think about the angels—the whole world lights up, and all sorrows and fears are gone.

Giving a Belated Christmas Present

Hans Jurgen Hauser

While I was attending the Fall Festival at Mountainview Family Church, San Tan Valley, Arizona, in October 2010, I walked over to talk to my teenage friend named Christian Morris. While I was talking to Christian, I noticed a teenager with dark hair and brown eyes. I asked Christian, "Who is this person?"

"Oh, this is my friend, Jake Harms," he replied.

"Well, it is a pleasure to meet you, Jake." We shook hands.

"So, Jake, do you attend this church?"

"I don't hardly attend because I have to work on Sundays," he said.

"What kind of work do you do?" I asked.

"I am a landscaper," he answered.

"Well, Jake, I believe in the power of prayer, and I will pray that God will make a way for you to attend this church on Sunday," I said.

In late November 2010, I approached Christian and told him how I was impressed meeting his friend, Jake Harms.

"Well, Hans, I have great news, Jake will be here at the 10:00 a.m. service," Christian said.

"He is? Well, praise God!" I responded with joy.

When the 10:00 a.m. service began, I sat in the second row. When Jake approached the front row to sit with Christian, he noticed me, smiled, and we shook hands. When the service was over, I walked up to Jake and said, "Hey Jake, it is so good to see you. I see you finally made it to church."

"Well, I am out of work now because my boss got into an accident with the truck," he answered.

"I'm sorry to hear that, but I hope to see you soon," I told Jake. He smiled in return.

When I left the church that day, I rejoiced of how God answered my prayer in the most unusual way. Since Christmas was soon approaching, I decided to give Jake a present, that is my two self-published novellas entitled *Suddenly Stranded* and *Joe's Warriors*. When Christmas Eve 2010 arrived, I saw Christian at the church and asked him about Jake. He told me that Jake will be coming to the last service. Unfortunately, he never came. I took his present home with me and saved it for another time.

In the summer of 2011, I signed up to be part of Facebook. While I was browsing through Facebook, I typed the name Jake Harms and within seconds, his photographs appeared on the screen. I was so thrilled when I saw this. I immediately submitted a message to Jake requesting his mailing address. I waited a week for a response but received none. So, I submitted another message and again, no reply.

When I saw Christian at church, I asked him about Jake and his whereabouts. He told me that he and Jake will be having a sleepover at his house. So, I immediately wrote a letter to Jake and handed it to Christian. I waited months for a response but still no reply.

I took Jake's Christmas present to church on Christmas Eve 2011, but to my dismay, he never came. When I came home after the service, I put Jake's present in my closet feeling ashamed of chasing a vanishing friendship.

On the morning of March 25, 2012, I woke up with a nasal decongestion. I didn't feel like going to church that day. A while back, I heard a preacher once state, "If you are sick, church is the best place to be." With that statement, I decided to attend church and took a package of Halls cough drops to ease the pain.

When I arrived at the 10:00 a.m. service, I didn't feel like participating in praise and worship. What came to my mind was healing testimonies that I had heard a while back. As believers were praising and worshipping God, they instantly received their healing. So, I decided to do this. When that was done, one of the pastors preached the morning message concerning serving others, regardless of the circumstances.

When the service was nearly over and just before the pastor began to pray, I got up to go to the fellowship hall. While I was leaving the sanctuary, I saw Christian Morris standing with someone who looked familiar. When I got outside of the sanctuary, I asked myself, *Was that Jake Harms?* So, when the service concluded, I walked back into the sanctuary and approached Jake Harms. We exchanged greetings. I told Jake that I had a present I've been wanting to give him since Christmas 2010, and asked for his address.

The next day, I mailed my belated Christmas present to Jake. This experience reminded me of Robert Schuller's famed slogan, "Never Believe in Never!"

The Stars Appear

Kathleen (Kathy) Talbott
Written when she was 10

The stars appear

As snowflakes

Just

About

To

Fall

Until the morning sun

Melts them away.

Christmas 2012

Barry Jones

Christmas 2012 stands out as one of the most difficult times I have experienced.

On December 18, my oldest granddaughter, Ericka, was hospitalized with a wound on her left foot and a fever. After tests were run, she was diagnosed with osteomyelitis, an infection of the bones in her foot. Only two bones were unaffected.

Having been suddenly paralyzed at the age of 13, Ericka has walked through some tough times physically. Having been hospitalized countless times with infections, she has had long term treatments of antibiotics in various hospitals and at home, numerous surgeries, and wound care. In spite of all she has experienced, God has been faithful and healings have manifested. She was able to walk with braces and feeling had been restored down to her knees.

Ericka's team of doctors consisted of a primary care physician, a surgeon, and a specialist in infectious disease control and wound care. After conferring with them, it was time to make a decision. Would she go through another round of long-term antibiotics and wound care or would she choose to have an amputation?

There was no question about what the decision would be if left up to me. We had seen God work mighty miracles on Ericka's behalf over the years. After all, this was the season of miracles. My choice was to go the antibiotic-wound care route. I had faith to believe that God would heal her again. As a matter of fact, I had enough faith for myself and everyone else.

It was not, however, my decision to make. Ericka decided that the best choice for her was to have the amputation. She said that she was tired.

My heart hurt. I think that at least part of my disappointment was in the fact that we had fought so hard to avoid this very thing for such a long time. Now here it was, staring us in the face.

I had several family members who had experienced amputations in the past. All but one ended up having several surgeries. By this time, they had also all passed away. I didn't want that for her.

Once her decision was announced, both Ericka's mother and father agreed that an amputation appeared to be the best solution. While I hated to see it happen, I chose to remain as supportive as possible.

Surgery was scheduled for Monday, December 24. Yes, Christmas Eve day. Of all days for it to happen, did it *really* have to be that day? No. For some reason, the surgery was rescheduled for December 28. *Thank You, Lord.*

Needless to say, we celebrated Christmas at the hospital. At the top of Ericka's list of gifts received was the arrival of her father on Christmas Eve day. He resides in Florida and would not allow any of us to tell her he would be there for the surgery, as he wanted to surprise her. Surprised she was! When she saw him she cried out, "Oh, my dear Lord Jesus, have mercy on me," and she burst out in tears. The rest of us got a good laugh out of that and continue to tease her about it.

Ericka had a great support system. The day of the surgery she was surrounded by her mother, father, other grandparents and aunt. I chose to go to work, but that day and during the rest of her hospital stay, I would go to the hospital after work and spend the night and weekends with her.

My foundational Scripture is Romans 8:28 NKJV, *And we know that all things work together for good to those who love God, to those who are the called according to His purpose.* I had to continue to trust God to work it out, even though Ericka's outcome wasn't what I wanted it to be.

Although there were some bumps along the way, God not only gifted us with a successful surgery, but Ericka was fitted with her prosthesis in six weeks. Her health has improved, and she is able to walk with the assistance of a cane.

One result of this experience is that Ericka's relationship with the Lord has been strengthened. It has also allowed me to be more appreciative of the fact that while God doesn't always give us what we think we want, He does always provide us with what's best for us. All we need to do is remain open to Him and continue to trust Him.

Occasionally, I think of the original Christmas gift, given to each of us in the person of our Lord and Savior, Jesus Christ. I think of all that He suffered in obedience to God the Father that we might be reconciled to Him. Then, I realize that perhaps Christmas 2012 wasn't that difficult after all.

Journey Through the Storm

Debra Fitzgerald

The snow fell steadily in Akron as we began our drive to southern Ohio. It was a week before Christmas. The wind blew through the naked trees, yet the snow clung to the branches and accumulated.

My heart and mind felt numb as I reflected on the conversation with my younger sister, Mary, and our mother.

I had picked up the phone while I wrapped presents for my one-year-old son, Daniel, and my precious husband. I heard sobs and muffled cries from Mary on the other end of the line.

"Bob has been in an accident," were the only words I could understand. My mother took the phone from Mary and blurted out, "Yes, Bob has been in a terrible truck accident, and he didn't make it."

My mind tumbled with troubling thoughts as my husband, son, and I drove the three hours to Marietta. It was almost Christmas. Why did troubles erupt during this joyful season? The Lord felt far away—I could not feel His presence. What could I say to my five-year-old niece, Kayla? Her beloved father was gone. What about my sister, Mary? She had lost the love of her life, the father of her adorable daughter.

What about her relationship with Christ as her Savior. Would Bob's death put another obstacle in her path? Reality struck—*Mary is now a widow and a single parent.*

The Lord spoke to me when I cried out to Him. "There is an appointed time for everything—a time to give birth, and a time to die" (see Ecclesiastes 3:1). His presence revealed to me that He would be with me. Peace swept over me after the prayer, but I still did not understand why God had allowed this to happen. In an act of sheer will, I agreed to trust Him every step of this difficult journey.

After the memorial service, we continued to love my relatives through the suffering. I prayed that the Lord would bring good from this tragic death. However, I am not able to say how all these things fit together in God's perfect plan. We may not know until we reach heaven.

God faced a greater loss when He sent Jesus to be our Savior. He left the glories of heaven and was born in a humble abode. The plan was for Jesus to take the penalty of death on the cross for each one of us. His present was Jesus. And through His Spirit we experience "His presence."

Guiding Star

Karen H. Whiting

Bring one and all to come see the reason why
The star shines on top of the Christmas tree.
Beneath the tinsel and the glitter draw nigh;
See the newborn King in a humble stable!

A star, a star shining brightly in the sky!
One star shone above for all to see,
Only a few men chose to follow, but why?
For that star led wise men to Jesus, our King.

Don't just follow stars and to God say goodbye.
Choose to follow the One who made the stars!
Let Jesus be the star you choose to live by.
It's your choice—be wise, and choose to follow Him!

Merry Christmas, David

Jean Davis

Six months after our daughter, Libby, was born, I found out I was pregnant again. Our other children were not quite three and ten. Active in our church and involved with my husband's rural veterinary practice, our life was busy. How would I take care of two infants in diapers?

As soon as I knew I was pregnant, I began talking to this child and praying for him. Though we had decided on Libby's name a few weeks before her birth, I went into labor with the older two children with a long list of first and middle name combinations packed in my overnight bag. We decided on names for Molly and Sam after we saw which potential name fit best. But I knew right from the start of this pregnancy that this child was male and his name would be David. How could I name him David since our last name is Davis?

I talked to him in utero just as I had when pregnant with Sam, our middle child, who seemed to come out of the womb as a talker. Would David be an extrovert, too? Sam would sit in his high chair at dinner and chatter to his dad long before he was able to form intelligible words. Would our baby have brown eyes like mine, Molly's, and Sam's, or green eyes like my husband's and Libby's? Two boys and two girls meant our family would be balanced.

A few weeks into my awareness of this new life growing inside me, I began to have complications, then miscarried. Shocked and disappointed, I felt numb. "We have three healthy children," my husband said. "Be glad for that." I didn't want to seem ungrateful, so I packed my grief away with the hopes and dreams for this little one.

Four years later when my doctor said I needed to have a hysterectomy, I drove home after the appointment, locked myself in the bathroom, and cried. Actually, I wailed as I slid down the wall and collapsed in a heap. "David! David!" I sobbed. I hadn't thought much about the miscarriage in probably, well, *four* years. I didn't particularly feel the need for more children at that stage in my life. My husband was in school again, and I was working to support our family. Our life was complete, but my uterus was where our fourth child had lived for twelve or more weeks. My womb had been his home, and I was losing connection to him.

A friend explained that when his wife miscarried, they both grieved for the full nine months. That was the permission I needed. For the months following surgery, I grieved losing part of myself— my uterus (which I admit that, after surgery, I didn't miss)—and for the loss of the baby I didn't have. David was the child we didn't talk about, but with the anticipation of surgery, the floodfinally opened and I was able to feel the heaviness of loss. What I know now is, if we don't grieve our losses when they occur, grief accumulates. Our grief may become displaced, but we'll still have to grieve.

For Christmas that year, I bought a few new ornaments for our tree. Though I don't remember now what I purchased for each family member, I do remember being drawn to a small porcelain ornament of a teddy bear wearing a red cap and red sweater. The bear held a small gold frame. I felt a gentle peace as I bought the ornament to honor the babe that still lived in my heart. I hung the tiny bear with the rest of the ornaments on the tree. The frame held no photo, but it helped me remember.

"Merry Christmas, David," I said as I hung the sweet bear.

"Mama, who's David?" Libby asked. After I explained to her about the miscarriage, she said, "Aw, we had a baby brother? I always wanted a baby brother. I miss him."

Finally David was where he belonged—part of our family history, acknowledged, and much loved. I've remembered him all these thirty-plus years, especially at Christmas. He is in safe keeping until I make my way Home. Because of the birth, death, and resurrection of Jesus, I have a living hope. I know I will see David.

Three Christmas Wishes

Wilma S. Caraway

As we stepped out of the car on a cold December day, there it was in front of the court house . . . the tallest and prettiest Christmas tree we had ever seen. It set a festive mood as it stared down Washington Street where three little girls were about to do one of their favorite things—go Christmas shopping.

My sister, Rilla, and our cousin, Margie, had our little purses in hand. We each had five dollars with which to buy our gifts. We skipped down the street among the bustling shoppers to McClellan's, the local five and dime store, and bought beautifully colored wrapping paper and ribbon. That took a chunk of our money, but we loved making pretty packages for the ten-cent gifts we bought for everyone on our list. When we finished shopping, we went looking and wishing for ourselves, hoping that Santa would soon be paying us a visit and bring us wonderful presents.

With our packages in hand, we strolled down the sidewalk, glancing at the Nativity scenes in the brightly decorated windows of Joe Weisman and Company, the Neiman Marcus of Marshall, Texas, *and* the most expensive store in town. Although we were young— Rilla, ten and Margie and I, eight—we knew exactly where the toys were at Weisman's, the second floor. We scampered through the store trying not to bump into other shoppers as we made our way to the elevator. I suppose the lady operating it sensed we were scared to ride the elevator, because she smiled sweetly at us and said, "What floor, young ladies?"

"Two, please," Margie answered.

We stepped inside and up, up we went. The elevator stopped with a jerk on the second floor, and we almost lost our balance, causing us to giggle with delight. The door opened and there it was—the toy department—stocked to the brim with toys for boys and girls. It was an awesome sight.

We scanned the cars, trucks, books, trikes, and bikes. But we had one thing on our minds, dolls. We went straight to the dolls, dolls of all shapes and sizes. They were the most beautiful dolls we had ever seen! We held them, danced around with them, and then we each chose the one we liked best. Margie chose a doll with a blue dress and hat that matched her blue eyes. Rilla and I continued picking up dolls and putting them down until we found two that looked like twins except the one Rilla wanted had a blue dress, bonnet, and pinafore. The one I thought was the prettiest had a pink dress and bonnet. They all had pink lips, rosy cheeks, brown hair, and best of all eyes that opened and closed. We held our coveted dolls and were having a wonderful time until the saleslady approached us and said in a rather demanding voice, "May I help you girls?"

"No. No thank you, ma'am. We are just leaving."

We were frightened! We had spent all of our money, so we carefully placed the treasured dolls back on the shelf. We turned and dashed to the elevator as fast as our little legs could carry us. We ran through the store ignoring the warnings of the people, "y'all stop running in the store!" We rushed outside and jumped into the waiting car with Auntie, Margie's mother, at the wheel.

"Whew! That was close," Rilla said.

On the way home, we talked non-stop about the dolls as we described each one in detail. Auntie dropped Rilla and me off at our house and said, "See you soon."

"Thank you, Auntie, for taking us Christmas shopping," I blurted.

"We had a wonderful time. Thanks." Rilla said.

Mother came to the door and called out, "Aren't you coming in for coffee, Inez?"

"No, Aurie, not this time, but we'll be back in a little while."

Rilla and I didn't waste any time telling mother about the lovely dolls we saw at Weisman's. We said in unison, "We are going to ask Santa to bring them to us."

"Now don't get your hopes up," Mother said. "You know it's better to give than to receive."

Even though I was young, I realized we did not have a lot of money because I had five siblings, and there was the possibility that Rilla and I may not get those beloved dolls. But, on the other hand, I didn't think Santa worried much about money.

Days passed and soon it was Christmas Eve. We could not forget the special dolls that we had picked out. The three of us prayed that Santa would bring them to us. Christmas morning came and there was so much excitement when Rilla and I looked under the tree and behold, there they were, the two adorable dolls we had prayed for. We couldn't believe it! We were *so* happy, we jumped up and down with joy. I picked up my doll, clutched her to my chest, danced around with her, and cried, "Santa brought just what I wanted. Santa brought just what I wanted!"

Rilla chanted, "I can't believe Santa brought the dolls. I just can't believe Santa brought the dolls, but I'm glad he did."

Mother and Daddy looked at our prized dolls with big smiles on their faces. Mother said, "These *are* beautiful dolls."

Later on Christmas day, Auntie and Uncle Herbert came over for dinner. Margie hopped out of the car screaming, "I got her! I got her! I got just the doll I wanted, and I named her Ann."

Needless to say, we kids made a play house and played with our cherished dolls all afternoon.

And yes, Jesus does love the little children, and He knows what's in their young hearts and understands their simple prayers. He also knows as they mature in their knowledge and love of Jesus Christ, their prayers and faith will increase.

What a wonderful Christmas memory this is of three little girls in the early 1940s. I enjoyed reliving that childhood experience. My faith and love of Christ has definitely increased over the years as well as it has for both my dear sister and cousin.

Wilma Jean Shepard
with her Christmas doll

So . . . This Is Christmas

Steve Toney

W ell, I guess I really *Blue Christmas* this year. It was Christmas
Eve night, and I had worked all day. I had to go to the mall
to do a little last-minute shopping. I did not enjoy one minute of it, I
have to tell you. First of all, there's just no *Joy to the World* any more.
Everywhere I go, those *Jingle Bells* are just so dadgum noisy. And then
on every street corner, folks are standing there ringing those little *Silver
Bells*. Drives me so crazy!

And while I was walking through the mall, there was this little
church group singing, *We Wish You a Merry Christmas*. And every time
they sang "wish," *The Little Drummer Boy* would take a mighty swing
at his cymbals with both drum sticks. Well, the little bum lost one of
'em in mid air; and guess where it went? THAT's RIGHT! Hit me
right in the mouth! And now *All I Want for Christmas is my Two Front
Teeth*. I wanted to yell at him, *"Here Comes Santa Claus,* and now you're
on the naughty list." *O Holy Night!* I was so mad! It's a cinch no one
is going to be standing under the *Mistletoe and Holly* with ME now.

Anyway, my grandmother lives just across town. And so after I
had finished my shopping (plus an hour in the first aid station at the

mall), I went *Over the River and Through the Woods to Grandmother's House.* I didn't want her to be getting *Nuttin' for Christmas.* So I wanted to bring her some *Pine Cones and Holly Berries* to decorate the mantle over her fireplace. Well, when I got there, she had been drinking eggnog, and *Rockin' Around the Christmas Tree,* if you know what I mean. And now, she wasn't feeling too well. So she asked ME to *Deck the Halls. Ave Maria!* I couldn't believe it.

I went out to the porch where she had gathered *The Holly and the Ivy.* I was thinking, "Now isn't THIS *The Holiday Season?*" But I plowed on through *The Twelve Days of Christmas* that it took me to get her place where *It's Beginning to Look a Lot Like Christmas!* All the while, I kept thinking, "It's okay, *I'll be Home for Christmas.*"

Finally got done over there and headed back home. I guess the weather men from here to the North Pole must have been praying *Let it Snow! Let it Snow! Let it Snow!* I could have built *Frosty the Snowman* with just the snow that was on my windshield. It was such a white-out, I must have been having a mirage. I think *I Saw Three Ships* going down Main Street. By the time I got to my house, I knew I wouldn't be able to get my car in the driveway, without shoveling snow for the next few hours. So I just parked on the curb and began *Walking in a Winter Wonderland,* which HAD BEEN my front lawn just a little while ago.

I must say, while *It's the Most Wonderful Time of the Year,* and I HAD been dreaming of a *White Christmas,* I was ready to get all snug in my bed and take a long winter's nap. I knew there would be no one at my house to sing *Merry Christmas Darling* to me, and this was not my *First Noel* alone either. But I sure did wish for someone at *Home for the Holidays* with me. But there was no one except my two cats.

At least *The Friendly Beasts* would curl around my feet and keep them warm while I slept.

I put some Christmas music on the stereo and began to settle down for the night. Or so I thought. Just as I was nodding off really well, I heard some terrible racket. I sat straight up, and my cats were looking at me like, *"Do You Hear What I Hear?"* I ran to look out the window, and there was that ridiculous *Rudolph, the Red-Nosed Reindeer.* He was buzzing around over my house in the middle of the night with his nose so bright. The next thing I knew, I was *Dashing Through the Snow* trying to catch him and put his lights out. And some fat old guy in a red and white suit was standing on top of my chimney, yelling, "You better watch out. You better not cry, 'cause *Santa Claus is Coming to Town!"* And some perky little female elf was up there with him too, sitting in the sleigh, waiting for him, and singing, *"Santa Baby,* hurry down the chimney tonight." Well, I wasn't going to let that fat guy try to climb down MY chimney. He'd probably break it wide open and cost me a fortune. So I threw on my robe and my slippers, and I went *Up on the Housetop* with *Jolly Old Saint Nicholas.* Now, I know it *T'was the Night Before Christmas;* but I had NOT been saying *I Want a Hippopotamus for Christmas;* and trust me, that's about how big he was, too. I didn't really aim to be *Mr. Grinch,* but I also didn't need this guy taking a *Sleigh Ride* on my roof. Nor all eight of his tiny, stinky, nasty, ugly little reindeer pals (nine counting his little girlfriend) doing the *Jingle Bell Rock* up there, either! So I told him to get the heck out of there, and *Let There Be Peace on Earth.*

I guess he understood. And maybe he wasn't even too mad at me for the way I acted, 'cause as he took off, he yelled back at me, *"Have*

Yourself a Merry Little Christmas!" I went back to bed hoping the rest of this night would be a *Silent Night*. I snuggled in under the covers and told my cats, *"Sleep Well, Little Children*. After all, *Christmas is Coming* and soon we'll have *Chestnuts Roasting on an Open Fire."*

Before I knew it, *I Heard the Bells on Christmas Day*. Well . . . actually it was my front doorbell. A policeman had come to tell me *Grandma Got Run Over by a Reindeer*.

So . . . This Is Christmas.

My Christmas Eve Dream

Aurie Perkins Shepard Worden

Now I lay me down to sleep
From all harm, Oh, dear Lord, keep.

And on my pillow, so cozy and warm,
I dreamed the world was all a storm.

Swirling sand and timbers fell,
The world was dark as a deep, deep well.

I was so frightened I could not speak.
I tried to run but was too weak.

The wind whispered while passing by,
It said, "Look upward to the sky."

I raised my head and opened my eyes,
There was a window in the sky.

And in the window, I saw our flag,
It waved like never before.

And to its right a snow white dove
Cried, "Peace Forever More."

Awake, O Sleeper

Lori Ciccanti

Awake, O sleeper, and arise from the dead,
and Christ will shine on you.
Ephesians 5:14b ESV

And Mary said, My soul doth magnify the Lord,
and my spirit hath rejoiced in God my Savior.
Luke 1:46-47 KJV

During Advent season, I sometimes enjoy listening to the lovely plainsong music of Gregorian chants. One song in particular is known as the "Magnificat"—a reference to Mary's wonderful hymn of praise recorded in Luke 1:46-55. In this lovely piece, Mary skillfully weaves together a beautiful tapestry of Old Testament themes in a poetic expression of sacred worship. While skeptics may doubt that a young peasant girl from the lowly village of Nazareth could have written such a beautiful hymn, believers from every generation continue to be inspired by Mary's powerful testimony and demonstration of faith.

I imagine the first century church often sang Mary's *Magnificat* as part of their worship; other gospel hymns such as Zechariah's praise

(Luke 1:67-79) and Simeon's song (Luke 2:29-32) were no doubt sung as well. Less recognized, however, are remnants of ancient melodies incorporated throughout the New Testament. For instance, based on its literary style, scholars believe that Ephesians 5:14b above is part of the lyrics of one of those songs. In any case, it appeals for real adoration; an awakening of the soul through Him who moves our hearts to sing.

Reflecting upon Mary's song and the idea of spiritual awakening, I became intrigued by the prayerful mode and creative music of early Christians. The following is said to be one of the oldest non-Scriptural hymns, dating back to the third century, and entitled "O Gladsome Light":

> *Heavenly, holy, blessed Jesus Christ.*
> *Now we have come to the setting of the sun*
> *and behold the light of evening.*
> *We praise God: Father, Son, and Holy Spirit.*
> *For it is right at all times to worship Thee*
> *with voices of praise, O Son of God and giver of life,*
> *therefore all the world glorifies Thee.*

More than two thousand years later, God is still looking to put a song in the hearts of ordinary believers who earnestly desire to worship Him. Therefore, as Paul exhorts us, Awake, O sleeper! Let us wake up to the magnificent rays of heaven's Sonlight, and rejoice in the creative power of God's Spirit working in us. Then we too, will come alive, with hearts full of praise, to the glory of Jesus, whose miraculous birth we now celebrate.

Heavenly Father, quicken our spirits to sing Your praise and fill our hearts with the light of the glorious gospel of Christ. Put Your words in our mouths as we seek to proclaim the good news of our Savior's first advent, even while we wait in joyful hope for the blessed promise of His return. In Jesus' holy name, we pray.

There's No Such Thing as Small Obedience

Cheri Fields

Having confidence in thy obedience I wrote unto thee,
knowing that thou wilt also do more than I say.
Philemon 1:21 KJV

When we think of the Christmas story, we think of Mary and the angel, Elizabeth and Zacharias, the shepherds and wise men. Simeon and Anna have their places in the temple. And Joseph stands out for His swift and humble obedience to God's dream messages.

We know Joseph was called to provide for and protect Mary and her Little One: Jesus, God with us. But there was something else only Joseph could do to allow Jesus to please the Father.

"I am not come to destroy, but to fulfill the Law and Prophets." Jesus told His disciples (see Matthew 5:17). It was His flawless obedience to every one of God's commands and predictions which allowed Him to satisfy God with His sacrifice on the cross. But there was a paradox only Joseph could resolve.

Jesus had to be a new Adam (see I Corinthians 15:45), so the Holy Spirit took a daughter of David, Mary's human body, and created anew the Y chromosome to bring forth a stainless body for Him (see Romans 5:21). He is our brother, but without sin.

But this left two major problems. Without a legitimate father, Jesus would be expelled from the temple, unfit to join in the worship of the Father (see Deuteronomy 23:2). And the prophets had promised He would be a son of David.

Joseph couldn't be Jesus' biological father, but he had to claim Jesus as his own, or Jesus was automatically on the wrong side of both the law and prophets.

Joseph's obedience was simple, straightforward, and almost invisible. Only a few people during his lifetime ever knew what really happened (see John 6:42). But it was a vital part of Jesus' ministry. I look forward to shaking his hand some day in gratitude for his selfless sacrifice.

Our obedience won't affect every person who enters heaven like Joseph's, but it can make a difference for those God sends across our path.

Lord, my choices seem so small now. Help me to look to you each day so my life opens the doors for you to work miracles in this world. In Jesus' name, Amen.

Christmas Fellowship Makes Love Abound

Betty L. Ricks-Jarman

The Christmas season always excites me. By the time I pulled up in front of the restaurant on that crisp December evening, my excitement had intensified. I felt so happy knowing that this special day had finally arrived. Looking around the parking lot, I searched for a familiar face from church. Not seeing anyone, I eased into the nearest parking spot. It was 5:45 p.m. with fifteen minutes to spare. The banquet was scheduled for 6:00. It looked like I was one of the first guests to arrive.

Our church family arranged to gather here today to celebrate our annual Christmas Fellowship Banquet. Over the years, it evolved into a regular gathering built on a close-knit family and fellowship.

My pastor had made a reservation weeks in advance for use of the facility. Invitations went out to church members to get an appropriate response. A VIP invitation requested the presence of Jesus Christ as our special guest of honor. After all, He was the reason for the season and the center of our celebration.

When the idea of an annual Christmas fellowship first came up, the members all agreed. I thought it was a fantastic idea. As a single, older person, there were times when I felt utterly lonely and forgotten. That feeling became even more pronounced during the holidays when families came together. This Christmas fellowship filled my heart with boundless love—the spilling over kind. Sharing this time with my church family helped to take the edge off the loneliness.

As our pastor evoked the blessing over the food, we felt blessed and thankful for every blessing. I considered this time of fellowship as a special gift from my church family to me. I appreciated it more than they would ever know.

Celebrate

Karen H. Whiting

For God so loved the world
that He gave His only begotten Son,
that whosoever believeth in him
Should not perish,
but have everlasting life.
John 3:16 KJV

And God, in giving us His Son,
gave us so much more, and so we celebrate.
God, who like the evergreen tree
Gives us fruit in every season,
Invites all to be part of His family tree
Jesus came to show His love—we are His reason!

We celebrate the gifts unseen—
Stockings filled for each girl and boy
Remind us to be filled with the Holy Spirit
Enjoying Spiritual fruits and gifts of joy.

We celebrate the gift of light—
Tree light, starlight, soft candlelight,
Remind us to be like Jesus—light of the world,
Nearly 2000 years and His light still glows bright!

We celebrate the gift of joy
That winged angels came down to sing
Bringing everyone a message of glad tidings
We sing out this news with joy while Christmas bells ring!

We celebrate the gift of love—
God's love, always near and dear,
Reflected in wreaths of green, unending circles
The love that circles back to us, when shared all year.

We celebrate the gift of life—
The miracle of this child
One who reaches out offering eternal life.
We celebrate this Christ child, born so meek and mild.
We celebrate and give God thanks,
God who gives and gives again,
For our God who gave us Christ—our most precious gift—
We give thanks, for loving each child, man and woman!

Christmas Love

Christine Scott

L ove is a many-splendored thing, especially at Christmastime. You undoubtedly have been touched by the miracle of its special love. Young couples have a habit of becoming engaged at Christmas. For others, love often begins under a sprig of holiday mistletoe. Children fashion strange tokens of love out of old tinfoil, art paper, and bits of cotton. Somewhere, mixed with the messy glue and the garbled writing of a little one, is the message, "Merry Christmas—with Love!" It is probably the most beautiful card you will ever receive.

Love does not always come with hugs and kisses. Often it is wrapped in a gay package and tied with a bow. For some, it is in the loving effort put forth in preparing a holiday dinner. For others, it is the reward of a loving glance or a grateful smile.

Love is made of the strangest spells; it can perk you up or calm you down. Love sometimes makes you grab a child and hug him. They say that love makes the world go around, and I know for a fact that it sometimes makes you dizzy!

Love has an extraordinary potential. The more love you give, the more love you get, and the more love you get, the more love you give! When you figure out that statement, you will know the answer to the miracle of love. If you take love for granted, it will soon pass you by. If it is twisted, it will shrivel and die. Cherish love, and it will cherish you.

Love is linked to faith, and faith is linked to a star that led the Wise Men long ago. Centuries later, we are still touched by the circle of love that surrounded the birth of a child in a lowly stable. What a wide and wonderful circle it has become! May its peace and warmth touch your heart this Christmas and last throughout the New Year. It can happen, you know, because Christmas love is indeed, a many-splendored thing.

From Christine's book, *Vignettes of Small Glories* (Chapter: "More About Glories")

Budding New Year

Aurie Perkins Shepard Worden

We had a Merry Christmas
Every heart was light and gay.
Now we have a bright New Year
That is here with us today.

We will make no resolutions,
We don't keep them anyway.
Let's remember last year's blessings
On this Happy New Year's Day.

The New Year is like a flower.
It peeps like a tiny bud,
Hoping everything is fine
And we do the things we should.

Each month appears another petal
With a tiny peek to see,
If the sun is brightly shinning
As we hope that it will be.

When the petals on the flower
Reach the number twelve so fine,
All the petals then will fall
As we sing the new Auld Lang Syne.

Meet the Contributors

CANDY ABBOTT

Founder and director of Delmarva Christian Writers' Fellowship, author, publisher, inspirational speaker, and grandmom, Candy sees herself as a "fruitbearer." Compiling and publishing this book is a labor of love and evidence of her life's goal to exhibit the Fruit of the Spirit (Galatians 5:22-23) in all she does. She began writing in 1983, around the same time she co-founded Sisters in Christ, an interdenominational women's ministry. Candy directs the annual Fruitbearer Women's Conference, is a charter member of Southern Delaware Toastmasters, an elder and deacon with Georgetown Presbyterian Church, and executive director of Mothers With a Mission. She retired from Delaware Tech in 2001 after a 28-year career as Executive Secretary to the Campus Director. She and her husband, Drew, have owned and operated Fruitbearer Publishing LLC since 1999. They have three children and four grandchildren, all in close proximity to their home in Georgetown, Delaware.

You are invited to call Candy at 302.856.6649, email her at info@fruitbearer.com, or visit one or more of her personal websites:

www.Fruitbearer.com
www.FruitbearerEvents.com
www.FruitbearerWebServices.com
www.DelmarvaWriters.com
and www.MothersWithaMission.com.

Contributing Authors

Our sincere gratitude to the following members and friends of Delmarva Christian Writers' Fellowship for sharing their inspired words in this volume.

Gail Atlas – Gail's aim in life is to show who God really is, as best as mortal beings can understand Him. She finds great fulfillment as the children's supervisor for Bible Study Fellowship in Milford, as well as serving in church relations for Operation Christmas Child. She loves to read, write, and travel around the country with her semi-retired husband, Steve, in their RV. Gail lives in Seaford, Delaware. She and Steve have four grown children and nine grandchildren. You can contact Gail at makarios1225@yahoo.com.

Ellen L. Moore-Banks – Ellen is a Delaware native who lived in the Smoky Mountain area of Tennessee for six years. She began writing poetry in her teens and was first published in various church publications: the *Delaware News Journal, Mountain Press, News Sentinel* and *Tri-County News.* She wrote a monthly column for the Rocky Ridge and Greenhill Church of the Brethren, both located in Maryland. She is currently an active member of DCWF in Georgetown, Delaware, and resides with her husband, Linwood, in Ocean City, Maryland. Her current writing projects include a family cookbook, a children's book, and devotionals. The story of how she met her hubby has just been released in the book, *Memories of the Clayton,* the local movie theater in Dagsboro, Delaware.

Anna Buckler – Anna is fiercely in love with Jesus. She and her husband, David, have been married eight years and live in Blades, Delaware. They have ten grown children—five in Maryland, two in Massachusetts, one in Tennessee, and two in Florida. Her first published article appeared in the DCWF's 2012 *Christmas* edition. She worships at Victory Tabernacle Church of God in Laurel and can be reached at 302.262.0481.

Wilma Shepard Caraway – Wilma compiles quotes and writes articles, poems, and children's stories. Her book, *101 Surprises! Sayings with Scriptures You Didn't See Coming*, was released in September 2012. She is a member of Delmarva Christian Writers' Fellowship and hosts its annual writing retreat at Collins Pond. Wilma is an educator and lifetime honorary member of the Texas Parent and Teacher Association. Wilma resides with her husband, Elton "Lucky" Caraway, in Georgetown, Delaware. They have two children and two grandchildren. She can be reached by email at wiletc@comcast.net.

Lori Ciccanti – Lori enjoys sharing the Gospel through various forms of writing, teaching Bible studies, and raising awareness for the plight of persecuted Christians. Having a son with autism, she is also involved in ministries for the disabled. Some of her hobbies include reading inspirational true stories and devotionals, visiting historical sites, collecting dolls, and thrift shopping. Most of all, she enjoys spending time at home with her husband, Lou, three children, and two adorable cats. She can be reached by email at DLAlsina@mchsi.com.

Jean Davis – Jean has published devotions in the *Upper Room, Devo'zine, Cup of Comfort Devotional for Women, and Love is a Verb Devotional*. Her humorous and inspirational stories have appeared in *Vista, Live, FellowScript, The Heart of a Mother* and *Whispering in God's Ear*. She lives in Ocean View, Delaware, with her husband, Vergil. You may contact Jean by email at davis823@mchsi.com.

Cheri Fields – Cheri, of Delton, Michigan, is a pastor's wife, home schooling mom of five, and aspiring writer for Jesus. She was a contributor to the DCWF's 2012 *Christmas* book and is an active blogger. Interact with Cheri at www.creationsciencc4kids.com.

Debra Fitzgerald – Debra is a wife, mother, and grandmother. She works as a clinician/counselor with adults and children to overcome issues in their lives. She writes to empower and educate people by using her own experiences as well as others' to bring a message of the hope of Christ. While in California, she wrote a couple articles for *Teaching Home* magazine. In addition to writing, she enjoys reading and sewing. Debra encourages people who hurt to journal their feelings or express themselves through art and music. Her email is: dwffitzgerald@gmail.com.

Judi Folmsbee – Judi is a retired teacher after twenty-five years in special education classrooms. She has written three children's books. The second edition of *Bubba, the Busy Beaver*, was released in 2013. Her work has been published in anthologies, church booklets, and religious and secular newspapers. She enjoys photography, gardening, scrapbooking, family time, and her newest hobby, playing the banjo. Visit Judi at www.JudiFolmsbee.com.

Barbara Creath Foster – A former Delaware teacher and DCWF member, Barbara retired and moved to southwest Florida, where she lives with her oldest son. She's still writing and has completed two inspirational novels. She can be reached by phone at 302.227.2212 or by email at Barbara@storywriters.ws.

Faye Green – Faye lives in Middletown, Delaware. She has had three working careers: in the Prince Georges County, Maryland, school system, at Ft. George G. Meade working for the Department of Defense, and as a writer of poetry, fiction, and non-fiction. Her first book of poetry, *Labyrinth,* and a novel, *Dicey,* were published in 2013. Faye has a short fiction story, *The Boy on the Wall,* as a Kindle e-book, available from Amazon. She is a member of St. Paul's United Methodist Church, Odessa, Delaware, and Delmarva Christian Writers' Fellowship, where the Holy Spirit empowers and encourages through Christian fellowship.

Dan Hayne – Dan is an internationally-known speaker, minister, and author. His book, *Keys to Your Future,* was published in 2012. He has a broadly diverse background that includes being a musician as well as a radio talk show host. His passion is to unlock and release biblical truths that will help people experience added dimensions in their walk with the Lord. Dan, together with his wife, Ruth, founded DH Missions to assist members of the Body of Christ come into the fullness of their purpose. Dan and Ruth currently live with their son in Spokane, Washington. Visit Dan at www.dhmissions.com.

Hans Jurgen Hauser – Hans' writing background includes published articles in *Mesa Tribune, Journal of Christian Healing, Creation Illustrated, The Victory News Journal,* a book entitled *One Touch from the Maker,* and most recently, an article in *The Christian Journal.* He has also had devotionals published in *The Spiritual Voice* newspaper with a reprint of one of them in "The Gem." In addition, he is the author of two self-published novellas entitled *Suddenly Stranded* and *Joe's Warriors.* Hans can be reached via email at hjhauser8@gmail.com.

Betty L. Ricks-Jarman – Betty was raised in Federalsburg, Maryland, and now resides in Greenwood, Delaware. She loves writing essays and commentaries that speak to the African-American experience, social issues, and family-relationships. Many of her essays have appeared in local newspapers and church newsletters. Previously, she wrote a bimonthly column for the *Delaware News Journal* as a contributing writer in 1995-96. She also writes non-fiction and is now working on her memoir entitled, *No More Crumbs.* She retired from the Department of Transportation in 2005 and has since co-founded Vine & Vessels Christian Writers Fellowship. Betty's desire is to use her writing voice to inspire hope and change in the lives of her readers. A mother and grandmother, she worships at Maranatha Holistic Fellowship Church in Greenwood and can be reached at bettylj2@yahoo.com.

Barry A. Jones – Barry was born in Maryland but grew up in Dover, Delaware, and currently resides in Seaford. She has an Associate Degree in Biblical Studies from Logos Christian College and Seminary in Jacksonville, Florida. Barry completed master's level voice acting classes at Voices for All in Albany, New York, allowing her to fulfill her dream of becoming a voice actor. A wife, mother, and grandmother, relationships are extremely important to her. She is an ordained elder and former pastor. Although most of her career has been in the banking industry, she loves people and desires to encourage others to maximize their God-given potential through her life and writing. She may be reached by email at jonesagapegirl@aol.com.

Michele Jones – Michele lives in Delaware with her husband, Eddy, *Preacher Par Excellence,* and their pound puppy and stray cat. They are blessed with two amazing children and are the proud grandparents of three. As a writer, Michele thrives in those moments when ink touches the page and poetry is born. She writes with a purpose to encourage others to see just how awesome and amazing our God is! Her devotionals have been published by christiandevotions.us. She was a contributing author for the *Voice of American Mothers* anthology, *Mom to Mom,* and has published two books of inspirational poetry, *Dance as David Danced* and *A Call to Worship*. Michele would love to hear from her readers at wordpraise@gmail.com.

Sandy Jones – Sandy was born in Bridgeton, New Jersey, has degrees from Hougton College and Glassboro State (now Rowan University) where she majored in English. After four years of administrative work in the U. S. Air Force, she taught in a New Jersey high school, community college, prison, and New Mexico Girls' Ranch for teens at risk. She has traveled to most of the states in America, including Alaska, as well as Europe, the United Kingdom, Spain, Portugal, Japan, Thailand, and Hong Kong. She serves as president of Shepherd's Fold USA, a non-profit organization for an orphanage in Shepherd's Fold

India (www.shepherdsfoldfamily.com). She is also a certified facilitator for the Modern Day Princess Program (www.moderndayprincess.net). Sandy and her husband have one married son and a grandchild who is two and a half. Feel free to email her at 2sandjo@gmail.com.

Betty Lewis Kasperski – Betty is an educator, business leader, certified lay minister, writer, and inspirational speaker. Coming from a family of educators and business owners, she feels comfortable in a variety of settings, including public speaking. Her first book, *Severed Yet Whole,* was released in 2012. She holds a Master's Degree from Syracuse University and resides in Georgetown, Delaware, with her husband, Stephen. Visit Betty online at www.severedyetwhole.com.

Eva C. Maddox – Eva is a graduate of Wright State University and has taken courses in counseling and nursing as well as several Bible courses through her local church. Eva writes devotions, articles, poems, and stories and has recently completed her first novel. A number of her writings have been published in a variety of Christian publications. In July 2012, she began Kingdom Writers Fellowship, a Christian writers' group that meets monthly in Seaford, Delaware. You may contact her at evacmaddox@comcast.net or check her blog: www.maddoxmatters. wordpress.com.

Teresa D. Marine – Teresa is a single mom of two amazing teenagers, Erin and Jordan. She is a lover of the written word and faithful employee of eighteen-plus years at INTEGRA Administrative Group. She lives in Seaford, Delaware, where she has served in many capacities in her home church, Atlanta Road Alliance, including divorce care, children's church, and women's ministries. She can be reached at tdm4him@yahoo.com.

Cat Martin – Cat Stenger Martin is the wife of Jim Martin. She works as a volunteer peer in mental health recovery and has an active life as a mother and grandma. In addition to writing poetry, she finds fulfillment in ministering to the homeless. She's a member of Georgetown Presbyterian Church. Cat can be reached at faithandactions@hotmail.com.

CHRISTMAS PRESENCE

Peter Mires – Peter is the author of *Bayou Built: The Legacy of Louisiana's Historic Architecture*, as well as contributor to the *Encyclopedia of Vernacular Architecture of the World* and *The Delaware Adventure*. His nonfiction has appeared in various publications, including the *Delmarva Review*, *Geographical Review*, *Literary Traveler*, and *Nevada Magazine*. Peter grew up in Dover, Delaware, where his family attended Christ Church. He currently manages the bookstore at Delaware Tech in Georgetown and can be reached at pmires@dtcc.edu.

Kathryn Newman Schongar – Kathyrn is a native of Fair Lawn, New Jersey. She received her BS in Secondary Education from Keuka College, New York, before teaching English in Massachusetts and Ohio. After treasuring her time as a stay-at-home mom, Kathryn worked for the Avon Central School District in New York as a substitute teacher, a tutor for students in grades K-12, and an English as a Second Language (ESL) tutor. She did all this while earning her Master's Degree in Education from SUNY Geneseo. Kathryn retired to Peterborough, New Hampshire, with her husband so they could be closer to family. She has joined the Monadnock Writers' Group with plans to write more about her inspirations: her college mentor and poet Ralph W. Seager, her family, her students, and her life. Contact Kathryn at kschongar@gmail.com.

Rita Schrider – Rita lives in Selbyville, Delaware, with her husband, Bill. They enjoy spending time with their children and two grandchildren. She works as a nurse, but her passion, among other things, is writing. Rita is on an amazing journey finding peace and serenity through the Word of God and His love, which causes her to write from the heart. This is her first published work. In the future, she hopes to write and publish children's books and songs praising God's love. Her email is ritaschrider@yahoo.com.

Christine Scott (Boaz) – Christine Scott (Boaz) is a native of Pennsylvania. Her mother died during childbirth, and the doctors said that Christine would not live long and, therefore, should be placed in an institution. Her grandparents had great faith and said they would take the baby and raise her. Now, eighty years later, Christine resides in Delaware. She attended college at New Mexico Highlands University and lived most of her adult life in Maryland and Virginia where she retired from the corporate headquarters of the Navy Federal Credit Union. Guided by her previous background as a newspaper editor, columnist, instructor, inspirational writer, and speaker, she is a natural "story teller," sharing her life in short articles and in her book, *Vignettes of Small Glories*. She is the mother of Jeffrey Scott, who submitted her stories.

Sue Segar – Sue has a degree in Advertising Design from the Art Institute of Philadelphia. After working over a decade in print advertising, she became a stay-at-home mom. Sue and her husband, Tom, home schooled their two children from preschool through high school. Their son, Mike, graduated in 2013 and daughter, Sam, will graduate by 2016. Because of Sue's love for the Lord and everything positive, it is her hope that this, her first submission of written work for publication, is just the beginning of a call to encourage others by sharing her life experiences. Sue enjoys many activities, most of all spending time with her family. She has kept her freelance business, Segar Graphics, alive by doing various projects over the years. Her work includes: book cover designs, graphic illustrations, letterhead, and logo designs. Sue can be reached at Segar Graphics PO Box 53, Hillsboro, MD 21641, or by email at ses1506@verzon.net.

Joyce Sessoms – God has made provisions for Joyce, a retired educator, to launch the vision He gave her. As Director of The ARK Educational Consulting, Inc., she provides the opportunity for parents and students to develop strategies which will help reduce the drop-out rate in her community and provide resources and guidance for youth. Joyce co-directs Vine & Vessels Christian Writers Fellowship, established in 2007 to provide a forum for aspiring and seasoned writers to perfect their craft. Her first book, *SuccessAbility! Taking the Burden out of Navigating High School* was released in 2010. Joyce is a doctoral candidate at Wilmington University. She and her husband of 21 years, Furman, reside in Laurel, Delaware.

Together they have and adore their three children, seven grandchildren, and three great-grandchildren. Joyce can be reached at crownjewel777@comcast.net.

L. Claire Smith – Claire was born in upper New York. She and her siblings grew up in foster care. Although she started out to be a nurse, she soon discovered that teaching and writing were her true passions. A playwright for twenty-five years, she has also written articles and short stories for adults and children. Claire has a certificate of graduation from Bethany Fellowship Missionary Training School (now Bethany Missionary College), an Associate Degree in Science from Adirondack Community College, a Bachelor's Degree in Secondary Education English from the State University of New York in Oceonata, and has completed several post graduate hours. Now retired from teaching, she makes her home in Lincoln, Delaware. Her first book, *Choose to be Chosen*, was released in 2009. Contact Claire at klayre_smith@yahoo.com.

David Michael Smith – David writes from his hometown of Georgetown, Delaware, where he has resided his entire life. He solely credits God for his publishing successes, which includes several appearances in *Chicken Soup for the Soul, Cup of Comfort* and *Guideposts*. He also covets the faithful encouragement of his wife, Geri, and children Rebekah and Matthew. He writes to bless God's children. Contact David at davidandgeri@hotmail.com.

Deborah R. Sullivan – Deborah is a nurse by profession, with a Bachelor of Science in Nursing, a Master's in Public Administration, and certification in Legal Nurse Consulting. She began writing Christian poetry after accepting Christ as her Savior in 1984. Her first poem, "The Most Precious Gift," was an answer to prayer while seeking a way to witness to a loved one. She has produced greeting cards, note cards, and a collection of poems titled *Invitations to Christ*. Deborah lives in Milford, Delaware, with her Cavalier King Charles Spaniel, Higgins. Contact Deborah at P.O. Box 298, Milford, DE 19963, or by email at Invitatx2Christ@aol.com.

Kathleen Talbott – During her career of 34 years, Kathy earned her Bachelor of Arts from Shepherd University, Sheperdstown, West Virginia. She enjoys writing fiction and non-fiction, spending time with friends, reading, and gardening. Kathy and her husband, Travis, attend Crossroad Community Church and live in Georgetown, Delaware, where they live with two dogs and a parakeet. Kathy can be reached by email at tktalbott@msn.com.

Ruth Thomas – Ruth is a minister, a chaplain at Nanticoke Memorial Hospital, involved with the prayer shawl ministry for the patients, and teaches Bible study in the Cheer Centers in Georgetown and Roxana, Delaware. She enjoys knitting and writing and has a book of poems currently being edited as a book on prayer. She can be contacted at 302.339.3216, or rthomas45@comcast.net.

Mary Emma Tisinger – Mary Emma is a southerner, born and raised in the mountains of North Carolina, who now calls Delaware home. A graduate of Berea College in Kentucky, she also holds a Master's Degree in Education from the University of Delaware. Retired from the office and the classroom, she divides her time among family, church, and community service. Always a lover of words, she writes poetry, fiction, and non-fiction, and has been published in several magazines and church papers. She has also written program material for American Baptist Women's Ministries and has published a church history. She currently authors a newsletter for her club and is nearing completion of an inspirational gift book which she hopes to see published in the coming months.

Steve Toney – Steve and his wife, Debbie, live in Ovilla, Texas, near Dallas. He is retired and enjoys writing poems. "I love to write poetry and make my words rhyme. It becomes all-consuming, but I have a good time." He has written poems for his family and friends as well as short stories. Steve self-published a book titled, *Life's Little Gifts*. He can be contacted at 972.748.2575, or by email at steve.toney@att.net.

Karen H. Whiting – Karen is the award-winning author of sixteen books, including *Time, My Mini Dream Room, God's Girls* series, and *The 365 Most Important Bible Passages for Women*. Her writing experience includes more than 500 magazine articles in more than sixty periodicals. Karen is the mother of five, including two rocket scientists, and a grandmother. Her newest release is *The One-Year Princess Devotions*. Karen has spoken in such faraway places as Russia and Malaysia. She hosted the television series, *Puppets on Parade,* for Miami educational TV and has been a guest on various television shows. She served as a writer for Focus on the Family's parenting magazines until they ceased publication. *Stories of Faith and Courage from the Home Front* received the 2013 Military Writers Society of America Gold Medal in the faith category. The book also received the Golden Scroll Nonfiction Book of the Year at the International Christian Retail Show. Karen loves helping grow tomorrow's families today with her books for youth and helping today's families thrive. Visit Karen at www.karenwhiting.com.

Kristin Caraway Whitaker – Kris was born in El Paso, Texas, and has enjoyed living in many other places during her lifetime. She credits the interesting locations and many wonderful friends she has made in each place with helping her adjust to the many moves and changes along the way. Most recently, she spent two years in Okinawa, Japan, and is now living with her husband and their beloved cat in Schonaich, a small village near Stuttgart, Germany. Once the editor of her small town newspaper, the *Leader Journal* in St. James, Missouri, Kristin is now enjoying semi-retirement in Germany. She still writes stories and poems for eleven grandchildren and others, and takes photos of the great places that she and husband, Randy, visit every chance they get. She can be reached by e-mail at randyw20@att.net.

Aurie Perkins Shepard Worden (deceased) – *Poems submitted by daughter Wilma S. Caraway.* Aurie wrote poems throughout her adult life. The earliest poem on file is dated 1932, which Aurie wrote at the age of 18. By the time she was 30, she was the mother of six children, "Two adorable boys and four darling girls." She often wrote poems for her children's school assignments and other occasions. Some poems were published in the local newspaper. A picture of Aurie surrounded by her grandchildren and great-grandchildren as she read poems from her published book *Grandmother's Poems for Children* was featured on the Lifestyle page of the *Marshall News Messenger,* May 14, 1978, as a Mother's Day tribute to her by her children. During her lifetime, she wrote more than 200 poems. She attended the Delmarva Christian Writers Fellowship Retreat at Collins Pond in 2007, where she shared three of her favorite poems and later signed autographs.

May the Presence

of Christ Jesus

be Yours this Christmas

and Always.

Our Other Books

*C*__HRIST IS NEAR__
__*Advent Meditations*__ by Delmarva Christian Writers' Fellowship, was initially published in 2002 to give beginning writers an opportunity to see their work in print. Completely revised and re-released in 2011, this 36-page booklet offers devotions from the first Sunday in Advent through Christmas Day.

*C*hristmas is the heart and face of God. It is Emmanuel, God with us—the fulfillment of the voices of the prophets. The rough-hewn wood of the manger was the first step of our infant Redeemer toward Gethsemane and the stark cross on the hill. The story of Christmas is love expressed and hope fulfilled. May you experience all that is Christmas through the 242 pages of this collection of family-friendly short stories, devotionals, poems, and tidbits. After all, they are designed to reflect the heart and face of the One called Love.

All three DCWF books are available on Amazon.com.

For autographed copies, bulk discounts,
or information on
Delmarva Christian Writers' Fellowship
contact the publisher or visit
www.DelmarvaWriters.com

Candy Abbott
Fruitbearer Publishing, LLC
P. O. Box 777
Georgetown, DE 19947
302.856.6649
302.856.7742 (fax)
info@fruitbearer.com